Monarch

Butterflies

Monarch Butterflies

SAVING THE KING OF THE NEW WORLD

Phil Schappert

Stengl "Lost Pines" Biological Station,

Integrative Biology, University of Texas at Austin

KEY PORTER BOOKS

National Library of Canada Cataloguing in Publication Data

Schappert, Phillip Joseph, 1956–
    Monarch butterflies : saving the king of the New World / Phil Schappert.

Includes bibliographical references and index.
ISBN 1-55263-405-1

1. Monarch butterfly. I. Title.

QL561.D3S33 2004   595.78'9   C2004-903086-8

The Canada Council | Le Conseil des Arts
for the Arts | du Canada

ONTARIO ARTS COUNCIL
CONSEIL DES ARTS DE L'ONTARIO

The publisher gratefully acknowledges the support of the Canada Council for the Arts and the Ontario Arts Council for its publishing program. We acknowledge the support of the Government of Ontario through the Ontario Media Development Corporation's Ontario Book Initiative.

We acknowledge the financial support of the Government of Canada through the Book Publishing Industry Development Program (BPIDP) for our publishing activities.

Key Porter Books Limited
70 The Esplanade
Toronto, Ontario
Canada M5E 1R2

www.keyporter.com

Cover design: Peter Maher
Electronic formatting: Jack Steiner

Printed and bound in Canada

04 05 06 07 08 09 6 5 4 3 2 1

To Pat,
for her forbearance and support,
above and beyond the call of marital duty,

and

To Don Davis,
for his long service and dedication to the Monarch

Contents

Acknowledgments

Like my previous book, *A World for Butterflies,* this book would not have been possible without the support of a great many friends and colleagues. Larry Gilbert, Dr. Loraine I. "Casey" Stengl and Lorraine Wyer deserve special mention for fostering our stay at the Stengl "Lost Pines" Biological Station of the University of Texas at Austin. The station remains one of the best places I can think of to write a book (or two). My thanks also to John Abbott and Dan Petr for leading a truly satisfying and enjoyable trip to the Monarch sanctuaries and Mexico City—Pat and I will always remember this trip with joy.

Since 1995, when I first became involved with the Commission for Environmental Cooperation (the environmental arm of NAFTA, the North American Free Trade Act) to write a status report on the distribution and conservation of the Monarch butterfly in Canada, I have met many of the "movers and shakers" among Monarch researchers. My thanks and gratitude to all of them—you know who you are—for discussions, arguments, thoughts and guidance about understanding the problems Monarchs face today. I am also indebted, once again, to Don Davis, one of Monarch biologist Fred Urquhart's cadre of taggers, the Monarch's best friends in Canada.

My gratitude to Don Davis, Andrew Jones, David McCallum and Mike Quinn for taking the time to read and provide their comments on the manuscript—their help has truly enhanced the readability of the text. Thanks are due also to the photographers whose beautiful images are what make this a useful and wonderful book, and to Steven Price and the World Wildlife Fund (Canada) for providing both the opportunity and their confidence in my ability. Finally, to Anna Porter, Clare McKeon and Michael Mouland, and all of the folks at Key Porter Books, my thanks for once again supporting me, despite considerable delay, while I got this off my chest.

Early European settlers of North America were impressed by the magnificence of the Monarch's striking colors and called them "King Billys" after William of Orange, a Dutch prince who became king of England in 1689.

Preface

The Monarch is an unusual butterfly by almost any measure. Imagine, if you can, an entire generation of butterflies that undertake a journey *en masse* covering up to 4,500 km (2,800 mi) or more—to a place they've never been—in a last-ditch effort to avoid the travails of winter. Imagine also a generation that, on the whole, lives five to seven times longer than the generation that preceded it and waits all of that time to fulfill its one and only purpose—to reproduce—only to barely begin the journey back to where they came from before the vast majority of them die. Consider that compared to even its closest relatives, never mind butterflies in general, the Monarch has a very unusual sex life: it eagerly partakes of the chemical precursors of needed sex pheromones but rarely, if ever, uses them, preferring instead to aggressively coerce its mates rather than lure them with perfumes, overtures and courtship rituals. Imagine a single butterfly that accomplishes all of this and survives, storing potentially noxious chemicals it acquires from its milkweed host plants for its own protection, only to succumb to the predators that await it at its only safe haven.

A most unusual butterfly, indeed…

In this book, I will take you on a virtual journey through the seasons and across North America from central Mexico to Canada and then back again. We begin in the overwintering grounds of the Monarch, in a living cathedral of trees where millions upon millions of butterflies wait for spring, and then travel north by northeast with the breakup of the colonies as the butterflies move to begin recolonizing their former range.

We'll follow them as they seek out their obligate caterpillar host plants, the milkweeds, then spend some time in their breeding range with the generations that follow, shifting north and then south again with the seasons and the availability of host plants, learning how the Monarch copes with the trials and tribulations of everyday life as well as the pressures we exert on their lives. Finally, we'll follow the last generation of these butterflies as they delay their natural reproductive cycle, and journey with them, south by southwest, as they make their way back to their overwintering range.

While a plethora of books, articles and papers have been written about Monarch butterfly migration and the need to protect this endangered phenomenon, most—if not all—of them have focused on the overwintering roost sites in Mexico and California and virtually ignore what might be going on in the breeding range. Throughout my education (as an undergraduate at Trent University in Peterborough, conducting doctoral work at York University in Toronto and continuing well into my post-doctoral work and research here at the University of Texas), I have been consistently challenged to see all sides of a problem. I continually ask myself: is the glass half empty or half full? There are always two sides to every story and the conservation of the Monarch is no exception. My purpose with this book is to tackle and grapple with the *other* side of the Monarch story.

As we will learn, the entire eastern North American Monarch population does take refuge in only a few small areas of central Mexico. This, I think, gives entirely new meaning to the old adage about the danger of having all of one's eggs in a single basket. What worries me most, however, is that Monarchs are not secure—not by any stretch of the imagination—in their breeding range either. They are threatened in a surprising number of ways, and I will argue that those threats have a dramatic impact on just how many "eggs" are in those overwintering "baskets."

Yes, the survival of Monarch butterflies at the winter roosts impacts the potential size of the breeding population in any given year, but the reproductive success or failure of the subsequent generations of non-migrants also has dramatic effects on the number of butterflies that make it to the winter roosts. My central thesis is that you can't save one without the other.

Given that forewarned is forearmed, I hope that this book will open your eyes to these threats and thereby offer us a means of countering them. Lincoln Brower, acknowledged to be one of the leading Monarch researchers in the world, believes that the North American Monarch actually has a very poor chance of surviving through the next 20 years. The thought of losing this familiar but wondrous creature is sobering, to say the least. The Monarch is an amazing and unusual creature, and its phenomenal migration—amongst other things—make it absolutely unique, and, in my view, completely deserving of its royalty. While it appears to be secure and unthreatened—after all, since Monarchs can now be found in a number of places all over the world it is doubtful that they will ever truly go extinct—the Monarch is actually in far more danger here in North America than we might think.

Chapter 1

The King of
North America

What surprised me was how cold it was. Here we were less than 20 degrees north of the Equator—well within the Tropics—but as we trekked across the meadows and pastures toward the track that would lead up to the site at Sierra Chincua, we walked through the man-made fog of our own exhaled breath. Yesterday morning, as we had climbed the stairs at El Rosario, it had actually been down to freezing but this morning was warmer by a scant few degrees. Still, there was an abundance of easily recognized wildflowers—senecio, lupine and sage—and maidenhair ferns, too. They, also, were not at all what I expected to see.

We stopped partway up the soon-to-be-dusty track for a group photo, a dozen and a half intrepid explorers, some who came along to simply see before it disappeared, others to satisfy their curiosity, the rest of us to renew some half-remembered sense of wonder. Of course, it was the elevation that made it feel this cold. My brain knew this, but my brain and my heart seemed to be on different planets. The elevation was also obviously responsible for the recognizably temperate floral elements. The question that kept running, over and over, in my mind was "why?"

Why here? What possessed such a seemingly fragile creature as a Monarch butterfly to undertake the long perilous journey across unknown, untravelled distances to this place? None of the butterflies had been here before, yet those that survived the journey all found their way here. From places as far away as central Ontario, the Adirondacks, and the corn belt and prairies of the upper Midwest, they came and congregated here in the mountains of the Transverse Neovolcanic Belt, the Sierra Volcanica Transversal, of central Mexico. It was cold here. Of course, that in itself was part of the answer. The other half, however, was that it wasn't too cold here. This is just one of the many contradictions that make the Monarch butterfly— the King of North American butterflies—so enigmatic and unusual…

What's In A Name?

The Monarch butterfly is probably the most familiar and well known butterfly in much of the world. Brightly colored in a contrasting quilt of fiery orange patches with white- or orange-spotted black wing edges and black lines following the main veins of the wings, it is almost instantly recognizable. The familiarity of this audacious insect is reinforced by its common use in advertising, as a symbolic icon of all butterflies, and its selection as the official state insect of several U.S. and Mexican states. It is also a symbol of NAFTA, the tri-national North American Free Trade Act signed by Canada, the United States and Mexico during the late 20th century, an agreement that is wonderfully underscored by the natural distribution and migration of the eastern North American Monarch across the three countries.

Why would I call the Monarch butterfly, *Danaus plexippus*, the "King of North America?" Obviously its common name provides part of the answer, but there's more to this name than meets the eye. Gary Noel Ross, self-proclaimed "butterfly evangelist" and a great lover of all butterflies, once asked of the Monarch, "what's in a name?" Taking cues from renowned Monarch biologist and migration researcher Fred Urquhart, author and dedicated butterfly conservationist Robert Pyle and one of Dr. Urquhart's most stalwart, longtime migration taggers, Don Davis, Dr. Ross describes how the earliest European settlers of Canada and the United States, largely protestants seeking an escape from religious prosecution, were "impressed by the sight of such a magnificent butterfly" and named it—for its familiar orange and black color—after a well-loved prince of Holland who later became king of England, William of Orange. My own maternal grandmother often called them "King Billys" rather than "Monarchs," and this is likely the ultimate source of the common name.

The regal roots of this story run even deeper, because this particular King also has a "royal family" consisting of some relatives—the Queen, *Danaus gilippus*, and the Soldier, *Danaus erisimus*—and some courtiers including the very similar but quite unrelated Viceroy, *Limenitis archippus*. Note, even, the similarity of the Latin species names of these royal butterflies, a potential source of confusion to the novice. According to Chris Durden, Curator of the Invertebrate Collection at the Texas Memorial Museum in Austin, the scientific name *Danaus* is derived from a latinized form of the Greek *Danaos*, a historic figure who is purported to have led his people from Egypt to Greece, while *plexippus* was a mythological hunter killed by his own nephew. In other places our Monarch may be called the Wanderer, or simply the Milkweed Butterfly, but here in its native North America it truly is royalty.

The Royal Family Tree

The "royal family" of the Monarch, Queen and Soldier (but not including the oft-times mimetic, but quite unrelated, Viceroy) are milkweed butterflies, unusual members of an almost exclusively tropical and sub-tropical group of butterflies. The Danainae, regardless of whether they are considered as a sub-family of the much larger Nymphalidae (a family with multiple origins that includes as many as one-third of all butterflies, some 6,400–7,200 species) or as a subfamily of the Danaidae (a family that would only include them with the Ithominae and Tellervinae, or about seven percent of the Nymphalidae), consist of nine to eleven genera (*Amauris, Anetia, Danaus, Euploea, Lycorea, Idea, Ideopsis, Parantica, Tirumala,* and the relatively recently established monogeneric *Protoploea* and *Tiradelphe*) comprising around 160 species (*See table below*).

The subfamily Danainae is unified by a number of common characteristics that are not shared by most other butterflies. The caterpillars have smooth, brightly colored exoskeletons with pairs of tubercles or fleshy tentacles on two

The Subfamily Danainae (after Ackery and Vane-Wright, 1984)

Tribe	Sub-Tribe	Genus	No. of Species
Danaini	Amaurina	*Parantica*	38
		Ideopsis	8
		Amauris	15
	Danaina	*Tirumala*	9
		Danaus	11
		Tiradelphe	1
Euploeini	Euploeina	*Euploea*	54
		Idea	12
		Protoploea	1
	Itunina	*Lycorea*	3
		Anetia	5
		Total	157

The Royal Family, clockwise from top: the Monarch (Danaus plexippus)*, Queen* (Danaus gilippus)*, the mimetic but unrelated Viceroy* (Limenitis archippus)*, African Wanderer* (Danaus chrysippus) *and Soldier* (Danaus erisimus)*. There are more than 160 species of milkweed butterflies worldwide but the Monarch is most well-traveled—and most famous.*

to eleven body segments, and feed on the dogbane and milkweed plant families (Apocynaceae and Asclepiadaceae) although almost one-third of the subfamily (much of the tribe Euploeini) are also known to feed on the mulberry family (Moraceae). Adults are all boldly patterned, often in brown, orange, yellow and black, but some are strikingly marked in black and white or blue and black. All males possess abdominal hairpencils, scent-disseminating organs that can be extruded from the tip of the abdomen, while females share a unique foreleg tarsus that is clubbed and has four segments.

Almost 80 percent of Danaines are only found in the Oriental or Australasian zoogeographic zones, or realms, with a further 13 percent being found exclusively in Africa (the Ethiopian realm). In fact, the Americas, that is the Nearctic and Neotropical realms together, only have some 14 species, less

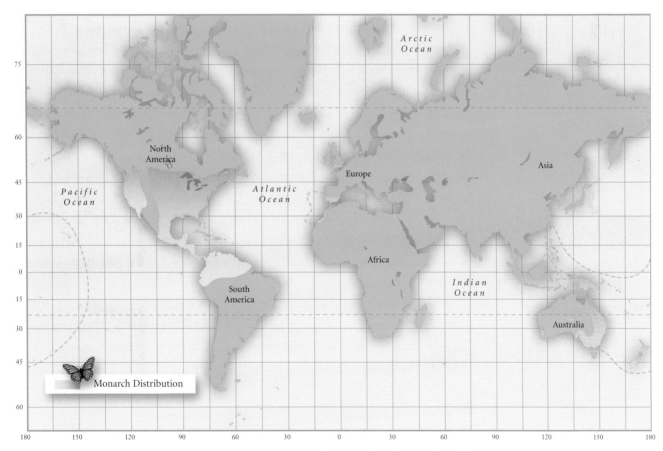

The worldwide distribution of the Monarch, Danaus plexippus. *The Monarch is found in five of the six recognized zoogeographic regions or realms for butterflies and moths.*

than nine percent of milkweed butterflies. Intriguingly, while three species are relatively widespread (and account for why the above percentages do not add up to 100) only the native American Monarch, the aptly named Wanderer of its old world populations, is found in five of the six realms.

In their book *Milkweed Butterflies: Their Cladistics and Biology*, Philip Ackery and Dick Vane-Wright further subdivide the genus *Danaus*, of which the Monarch is a species, into three seemingly well-delineated subgenera, *Danaus (Danaus)*, *Danaus (Salatura)* and *Danaus (Anosia)*. The subgenus *Salatura* contains four species (*D. ismare, D. genutia, D. affinis* and *D. melanippus*) that are exclusively Oriental and Australasian in distribution while the subgenus *Anosia* also contains four species (*D. erisimus* [the Soldier], *D. plexaure, D. gilippus* [the Queen] and *D. chrysippus*, the African Monarch or Wanderer) that are either American (Nearctic/Neotropical) or in the singular case of *D. chrysippus*, African (Ethiopian) in origin, although *D. chrysippus* is also now found throughout much of the Oriental and Australasian realms.

The subgenus *Danaus*, however, is exclusively American (Nearctic/Neotropical) and consists of the three remaining species, *D. cleophile*, the relatively rare Jamaican Monarch found only on the Caribbean islands of Jamaica and Hispaniola, the putatively separate species *D. erippus* of South America, found south of the Amazon Basin, and *D. plexippus*, the Central and North American Monarch. Unlike even its near relatives, the Monarch is now found in a wide variety of places, including its native Central and South America north of the Amazon Basin and the islands of the Caribbean, Hawaii, most of the larger islands of the Pacific including the Galapagos, Norfolk, the Solomon Islands, the Philippines and Taiwan, New Zealand and Australia, and is now also common in the eastern Atlantic—the Canary Islands, Madeira, southern mainland Europe and northwest Africa.

Milkweed butterflies are generally large, slow flyers that often glide on their expansive, outstretched wings for considerable amounts of time. Their caterpillars feed on plants with well-documented defensive compounds (cardenolides, or cardiac glycosides) that are sequestered and retained in the body and wings through the adult butterfly stage. Together with their bold colors and patterns, these defenses make them aposematic, or warningly colored, allowing them to avoid predators while flying or gliding in plain sight. Many Danaines also roost communally and are known to migrate short distances in some numbers. The Monarch, however, takes these traits to entirely new levels.

Life Cycle of the Monarch

Most researchers agree that the Monarch is a singularly unusual Danaine butterfly. It shares the southern portion of its eventual range with the Queen and the Soldier, which, although they may also be somewhat migratory (for example, the Queen was found through an impressive number of states in northeastern North America in 2001), rarely attain the population densities or expansive geographic range common in the Monarch. Intriguingly, the biology and ecology of the immature stages—eggs, caterpillars or larvae, and pupae or chrysalides—are very similar, as is their dependence on milkweeds, the importance of certain nectar sources to adults, and their bold, aposematic lifestyle. These similarities notwithstanding, the Monarch differs in enough important traits to be considered quite "unusual."

Eggs

Monarchs lay their eggs singly (as opposed to in clusters), generally on the upper leaves of a tender shoot of a milkweed (genus *Asclepias*) or sometimes a milkweed vine (genera *Cynanchum*, *Matelea* and *Sarcostemma*), all in the plant family Asclepiadaceae. There are approximately 110 species of milkweeds in North America, although not all species are used as host plants, and some species are preferred over others (or others are not suitable and avoided). Consequently, host use varies substantially.

Another significant factor affecting host plant use and suitability is the geographic and seasonal distribution of milkweeds. Milkweeds do not persist when temperatures are too cold or too hot, consequently there are no host plants available during the winter and milkweed distribution is limited by the length of the growing season in the northern parts of its range (presently above about 52°N latitude). However, during the summer the southern latitudes (below about 38°N) are also too hot for native milkweeds so plants are rarely found outside of the spring and fall.

Monarchs lay their eggs singly, usually on the upper leaves of the tender shoots of milkweed plants. Pale yellow or ivory when laid, the eggs darken to a gray-black as the caterpillar develops inside the egg, typically over three to eight days.

The eggs themselves are pale yellow or ivory when laid but darken to a dark gray-black, with the development of the caterpillar inside the egg, over three to eight days depending on temperature. They are taller than they are wide, flattened on the bottom where they are attached to the plant but with an apical point on the top, and have many vertical, faceted ridges.

The Caterpillar or Larva

Monarch caterpillars bear only two pairs of fleshy, non-poisonous "tentacles," tubercles or filaments on the second thoracic (metathorax) and eighth abdominal segments. The Queen, the Soldier and the African Monarch each possess a third pair of these appendages on the second abdominal segment, which makes it possible to easily identify Monarch caterpillars to species. These appendages are probably anti-predator devices since they contain body fluids, are mobile and can be waved about when the caterpillar is disturbed. The Monarch's minimum complement of these tubercles, placed on opposite ends of the body, likely also serve to confuse predators about which end of the body is the head and which is the tail.

Monarch caterpillars change from pale gray-white when freshly hatched to being brightly colored with alternating, complete, transverse bands of yellow and white on a black background. The yellow "bands" on the Queen and on the African Monarch, however, are incomplete and broken into "dashes" that do not completely encircle the body. The bright coloration, or aposematism, of these caterpillars is also an anti-predator strategy that advertises the fact that they not only feed on plants that contain noxious substances but that they have incorporated those compounds into their own bodies.

Monarch caterpillars prefer the top leaves of their host plant and are behaviorally "wired" to be negatively geotactic (they prefer moving upward against gravity) and positively phototactic (they also move toward light). The combination of these traits ensure that the caterpillars are highly visible so that their brilliant, aposematic coloration has the largest impact on potential predators. Further defensive characteristics of the caterpillars include their behavior of curling up and dropping off of their host plant when mildly stimulated and their ability to "foam at the mouth," regurgitating a cardenolide and ketone-laced foam from their mouths when they are continuously and strongly stimulated.

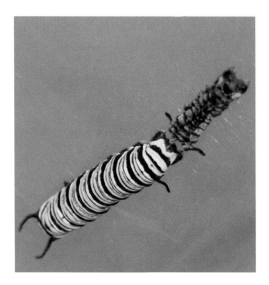

Monarch caterpillars grow quickly. In only 10 to 14 days, depending on temperature, the caterpillar will grow to more than 3,000 times its hatching weight. Caterpillars grow through five larval instars (periods between molts or shedding of their exoskeletal "skin," as seen here).

When caterpillar growth is complete, they usually leave their host plant to find a place to pupate. The prepupal stage has a characteristic "J" shape because the pupa or chrysalid will hang free, upside down.

Caterpillar growth and development is prodigious. Depending on temperature, a typical Monarch caterpillar proceeds through five larval instars (the periods between successive molts or shedding of their exoskeletal "skin") in 10 to 14 days, although it may take up to 40 days if temperatures are below 10°C (50°F). Within this two-week period caterpillars will grow from being about 2 mm (1/16 in.) long to being more than 3,000 times their hatching weight. One interesting characteristic of Monarch caterpillars is their penchant for basking in direct sunlight, a behavior that may reduce the duration of the caterpillar stage by enabling the caterpillar to raise its body temperature up to 8°C (46°F) above the ambient air temperature, thus allowing it to increase its metabolic rate.

The pupa hardens into a brilliant green chrysalis with metallic gold spots (top left). Depending on temperature, light and humidity, the pupal stage lasts from 9 to 15 days, after which the chrysalis will change color, darkening before turning translucent a few hours before the butterfly is ready to emerge (top right). An intake of air is used to expand and split open the chrysalis, allowing the butterfly to eclose, or emerge (bottom).

The Chrysalis or Pupa

Upon completion of the growth that characterizes the caterpillar stage, mediated by hormone balances, the caterpillar almost always leaves its host plant and crawls around to locate a place where it can pupate. It spins a silk pad attached to a branch or some other substrate, meshes its anal prolegs—hydrostatic leg-like appendages on its last abdominal segment that terminate in a pad of crochets or small hooks, not unlike the hook side of a strip of Velcro™—in the pad and hangs free, upside-down, in a characteristic "J" shape. It rests in this position for some time before the last larval skin splits along the top of the thorax (near the base of the "J") and the caterpillar shakes and gyrates to loosen the skin from the emerging pupal case or chrysalis. Before the old caterpillar skin is shaken completely off, the pupal cremaster, a special hook-like appendage, is securely fastened into the silk pad.

The Monarch chrysalis is a brilliant, but deceptively cryptic, green color with a line of metallic gold spots on a black background about two-thirds of the way up (at the junction of the abdomen and thorax) and a few gold and yellow spots at various places around the body. The function of these "gold spots" is not fully understood although some research has suggested that they may serve some organizing function promoting wing pigment development. Unlike some of its near relatives there is no color morphism in the pupa—that is, the chrysalis is always green—although an orange-colored recessive mutation has recently been described that further reinforces the Monarch's Danaine ancestry. Depending on factors such as temperature, light and humidity, the pupal stage lasts from 9 to 15 days, on average.

The Imago or Adult

Most milkweed butterflies are quite large and the Monarch is no exception. Their large size has a significant effect on their biology and no doubt contributes greatly to our perception and familiarity with them. Large wings with a relatively small body mass provide a high lift-to-drag ratio, aerodynamically speaking, that allows the Monarch to soar and glide for considerable distances—a very useful trait in a migratory species. Still, for all of their size, their wings are surprisingly flexible and Stephen Dalton's groundbreaking high-speed flash photos of a Monarch showed just how flexible they could be—capturing the wings as they seemingly "cup" the air, greatly increasing the efficiency of powered flight. The Monarch's large size also buffers

Adult Monarchs often cling to their old chrysalis for a few hours while their wings harden and they fuse the two halves of their proboscis. The brilliant orange and black color warns of the noxious compounds that they ingested as caterpillars feeding on their milkweed host plants. This aposematic warning coloration provides protection from predators that have learned to associate the color with the bad taste.

their thermoregulatory capability, or their ability to gain or shed heat, and they have developed behaviors such as "shivering" and anti-basking body orientation to respond to the effect that their large size has on their gain or loss of heat.

The fuel for the flight of the vast majority of butterflies is the sugar-rich nectar of flowers, and Monarchs have developed intriguing ways to convert and store these energetically needed carbohydrates as lipids (fats) in "fat bodies" within their abdomens. Of course, they also have the ability to re-convert these fats back into useable flight energy, another useful adaptation for both their migratory habit and their need to survive long periods of inactivity. Another useful feature of the conversion of sugars to fats for storage is that it increases body mass, thus lowering their lift-to-drag ratio and contributing to their "flight trim," or their efficiency as fliers. They've even developed ways to offset the use and loss of these lipids during migration by drinking and storing water to maintain their flight trim.

The use of noxious, cardenolide-containing milkweed host plants and the storage of these compounds in the Monarch's body are advertised by their brilliant orange and black coloration. Since the Queen and the Soldier also feed on milkweeds, they also advertise their unpalatability to predators in orange-brown and black patterns. Together, these butterflies are said to mimic each other to present a "united" color pattern that will "train" their vertebrate predators (birds and lizards) to avoid them. (*See "Monarchs and Mimicry" on page 14.*) This "co-mimicry" is called Müllerian mimicry after the researcher that suggested the hypothesis.

One final characteristic, the Monarch's unusual courtship and mating behavior, deserves mention. All male Danaine butterflies actively seek compounds known as pyrrolizidine alkaloids (PAs for short) from certain plants and nectar sources to produce sex pheromones. Males use these pheromones to "entice" females to cease flying and be receptive to mating. The pheromones are manufactured in glands in "alar spots" or pockets on the hindwings and are broadcast with hairpencils, extrudable brush-like organs from the tip of the abdomen that the males insert into their alar pockets to coat with pheromones. While Monarchs have alar pockets and hairpencils, visit PA-containing plants, and could court females in much the same manner as male Queen butterflies do, they largely choose not to but use coercive mating tactics instead.

Male Monarchs are larger than females, an unusual arrangement among butterflies where the female, who usually carries more mass in eggs and flight

MONARCHS AND MIMICRY

If we consider Müllerian mimicry's notion of shared pattern for protection, it makes sense that there might be "cheaters" who, even though they are not protected by any sequestered plant poisons, could be avoided by predators if they resembled a noxious "model." This "model-mimic" idea—where a palatable and unprotected butterfly can gain protection from predators simply by resembling a butterfly that advertises its chemical protection and unpalatability—was first proposed by Henry W. Bates after his observations of butterflies in the Tropics and has come to be known as Batesian mimicry.

The Monarch/Queen and the Viceroy have long been considered the "classic" example of this kind of model-mimic system. The Viceroy's appearance varies with its co-occurrence with either the Monarch or the Queen, and it was long believed that the Viceroy, which feeds on willow and poplar, was not protected by plant poisons. However, relatively recent research has shown that at some times and in some places the Viceroy is, in fact, just as unpalatable to birds as the Monarch or Queen. In other words, the Viceroy changes from being a Müllerian mimic of the Monarch and/or the Queen (unpalatable and chemically "protected") to being a Batesian mimic (palatable and unprotected) depending on the specific model species, their relative abundances and seasonality, the geographic location and the larval host plant of the Viceroy.

A further wrinkle comes from the variation in the presence, concentration and quality of the cardenolides or cardiac glycosides among Monarch host plants. Some species, such as the common milkweed (*Asclepias syriaca*), have low amounts of generally poor-quality cardenolides, offering little protection to the butterflies. However, enough individual Monarchs feed on other species—such as the green or spider milkweed (*A. viridis*) or the antelope horn milkweed (*A. asperula*)—that contain much higher levels of these poisonous compounds that a mimetic phenomenon, first described in Monarchs and dubbed "automimicry," occurs. As you might suspect, automimicry is an extreme form of Batesian mimicry in which highly protected individuals that have incorporated high concentrations of less palatable cardenolides within their bodies afford protection to more palatable, or less noxious, individuals within the same species.

The relatively rare "white Monarch" (Danaus plexippus form *nivosus), a genetic form with grey-white scales replacing the usual orange, bears a striking resemblance to some related* Idea *species of the Australasian realm. However, other than in Hawaii, White Monarchs rarely survive for long. This pale Monarch was photographed in Florida.*

muscles to support the larger wings needed to carry her, is generally larger than the male. Male Monarchs use their size and mass advantage to aggressively "attack" and subdue other Monarchs, grappling in the air and falling to the ground, where they attempt to mate. If successful in obtaining a copulation the male will carry the female to a shrub or tree to finish mating. An intriguing side issue of this tactic is that smaller males are often the target of attacks by larger males and male-male interactions among Monarchs are relatively common.

Origins

The Danaines are essentially tropical butterflies. Why then does the eastern North American Monarch travel each summer to higher latitudes, then return south each winter? Why do they choose to roost together and why roost in the mountains of central Mexico instead of the coastal rainforests? When did this annual migration begin? Unfortunately, no one knows the true answers to these questions, although there are some pretty good theories, and some corroborative evidence from other butterflies, including closely related species and details of what the Monarch does in other places. In any case, all of these questions lead, in one way or another, to the larval host plants, the milkweeds.

There are more than 100 species of milkweeds in Central and North America, although not all of them are entirely suitable as host plants. The most relevant fact about the native milkweeds of North America is that they are all seasonal; they die or rest through unseasonable conditions when it is either too cold and dry or too hot and dry to grow and flower. Host plant availability to the Monarch, therefore, is limited by the seasonality of milkweeds. There are no plants for caterpillars to feed on when it is dry and either too cold (winter in the north) or too hot (high summer in the south). But this is also true, at least in the winters of the northern United States and Canada, for most kinds of butterfly host plants. Why do most temperate species of butterflies overwinter, usually in immature stages (eggs, caterpillars or chrysalides), while Monarchs migrate away from the loss of their host plants?

For insight into a possible answer to this question we need to return to the Monarch family tree. It turns out that most of the Danaine butterflies have seasonal migratory tendencies, albeit on a much smaller scale than Monarchs, and many also roost together in overnight or seasonal roosts. For example, a number of *Idea* species are known to migrate to suitable habitats during wet and dry seasons in the Oriental realm and roost communally. Similarly, *Anetia briarea* individuals aggregate in roosts in the montane regions of the Dominican Republic. So the ancestors and relatives of the Monarch were already capable of escaping temperature extremes and, most importantly, the dry conditions in which their milkweed host plants perished by migrating to another area and hibernating in roosts. However, while this provides a possible *raison d'etre* for the southward migration, it doesn't explain the northward return.

For this we need to again consider their milkweed host plants. Milkweeds are, as their very name suggests, weeds that grow well under somewhat marginal conditions (although it's important to note that Monarchs seek out the plants that are in the very best condition because these will provide for the faster growth and best survival of the caterpillars). During the winter months, almost as far south as the Texas-Mexico border, there are very few milkweeds growing but as conditions get warmer and wetter the perennial species begin to regrow from their roots and the seeds of annual and perennial species alike germinate. This trend continues northward as the seasonal change from winter through spring progresses. (*See "Milkweeds and Migration" on page 42.*) It shouldn't come as any surprise that the breakup of the overwintering roosts in central Mexico coincides with the return of the milkweed to the southern United States. The Monarch "migration" north is, perhaps, better considered a recurring range expansion wherein the butterflies, over a couple of generations, gradually recolonize the entire range of available milkweeds.

Populations or Population?

Throughout this book I will be almost exclusively discussing the eastern population of North American Monarchs. I don't mean to slight the western populations, and the reader should realize that almost everything that I discuss in this book, from problems to population trends to Monarch biology, applies equally well to the western population, but I am far more familiar with the eastern population, it has a much larger range and population sizes are also much larger than its western counterpart. However, there are some additional differences, and even some controversy about whether there are one or two populations of Monarchs in North America.

One of the major differences between the eastern and western populations is that overwintering by the western butterflies is as diffuse as that by the eastern butterflies is concentrated. There are almost 400 known roosting sites along the Pacific coast of California in the United States (and even some non-coastal roosts near Death Valley) and Baja California in northwestern Mexico for the western population, while there are fewer than 20 consistently used roosting sites for the eastern population in central Mexico.

Despite this difference, the population size of the eastern population is much, much larger. One or two of the California roosts may reach as many as one hundred thousand Monarchs but most are much smaller and none approach the 20 to 30 million butterflies that may be found in some of the larger Mexican roosts. The total western population is at least an order of magnitude less than the eastern population.

The western roosts are also not as stereotypical as those of the eastern population, with roosts forming in a wide variety of tree species including pines, palms, oaks and the non-native *Eucalyptus*. It has been suggested that the planting of *Eucalyptus* trees has greatly increased the numbers of roosts available and caused the overwintering population to become fragmented and more susceptible to endangerment. Habitat loss through competition with man for coastal real estate is the single largest threat facing the western Monarch population at the roost sites.

Differences in population size and roost number aside, there are also a great number of similarities between the two populations. Both repopulate a breeding range and migrate to overwintering grounds in the fall. Both choose roost sites with moderate climates that buffer the extremes of severe cold and provide the proper moisture balance to sustain them. Both populations experience reproductive dormancy, that is they delay maturation and mating, and mate before colony breakup occurs in the spring, and so on.

Finally, while it has been widely held that the populations have always been entirely separate, recent thought is that the populations do share individuals from time to time and that there is a flow of genes from one population to the other and back again. Only a few years ago a number of Monarch biologists pleaded with the public to avoid "interpopulational transfers" of Monarchs from one population to the other, concerned that the movement of pathogens and parasites along with the butterflies could have a devastating effect on a susceptible uninfected population.

Recently, however, it has been suggested that in exceptional years the eastern population has "rescued" the western population through a large influx of eastern Monarchs migrating northwest instead of northeast. It is also probable, supported by some tag recoveries and the observations of Robert Pyle in his book *Chasing Monarchs* that some western Monarchs end up at the central Mexican overwintering sites rather than the coastal California roosts. While it is likely that some individuals from the two populations cross the Rocky Mountains, how much mixing or gene flow there is between the populations is unknown.

The stunning sight of millions upon millions of Monarchs, hanging from fir trees like so many autumn leaves, brings an ever-increasing number of curious butterfly watchers to roosts like El Rosario *in Mexico each winter. An estimated 120 million butterflies were found at all of the colonies in the winter of 2001–2002.*

CHAPTER 2

Living Cathedrals

SITTING ON THE WOODED HILLSIDE FAR ABOVE THE valley floor, directly across from the butterfly-laden firs, we too were waiting for the sun. We were just a few of the two or three hundred souls in one of the two or three viewing "galleries" at Sierra Chincua, waiting for a sign. As I had been the previous day at El Rosario, I was surprised but also somehow gratified by how many of the onlookers were Mexican. I had envisaged a mob of tourists with cameras, so seeing the local people visiting the sanctuaries impressed me to no end. As we sat and waited, along with the butterflies clustered on the trunks, branches and foliage of the Oyamel firs, I watched both the stunning sight of millions upon millions of Monarchs, resembling (if you didn't look too close) so many autumn leaves, and the nearly unbelievable sight of children playing and people talking, meeting old friends and playing cards as if they were off at some family picnic.

Personally, I was somewhat insulted. It felt like everyone was talking in church. The wonder of it all was a quasi-religious experience for me; it all but left me speechless and I thought "how rude, to be here amongst the firs with one of the natural wonders of the world, in a living cathedral of trees and butterflies, to spoil the moment by conversing in anything other than the hushed tones and whispers." The irony of the scientific name of the Oyamel, Abies religiosa, was not lost on me. As I leaned back to mention this to my wife, Pat, I watched a leaf fall off one of the branches above me and softly flutter down, waving gently, to land just inches from my feet. When I realized that my "leaf" wasn't a leaf at all—how could it have been, since the surrounding trees were evergreen firs, and not deciduous at all—but a butterfly, I quite forgot what I was about to say.

I reached over to pick the butterfly up and, realizing that it was still very much alive, placed it on my upraised knee, softly lit by a fleck of the rising sun. Within moments it began shivering and then slowly spread its wings out wide to *bask in the weak sunspot. It was a male and was in such good shape that it appeared to be almost freshly emerged, not at all the battered and torn, faded butterfly that I expected to see. After all, who knew where it had come from, how long its journey had been, how long it had been here, or even how old it was? Within another few moments—between the pale sunshine and the heat radiating off of my knee—it began to barely flex its wings, its wingtips tracing an arc that slowly increased in amplitude until its wings moved quite freely through almost 90 degrees, from the open basking posture to the closed position in which it had fallen off the tree.*

When someone called my name, I glanced over to see one of our trip leaders give me a come-along gesture. I gently picked the butterfly off of my knee and gave it to Pat with an admonishment to "take care of the little fellow," got up, glancing around somewhat guiltily at having disturbed the "service," and walked over to see what was up. Dan Petr, a colleague from Southwestern Adventist University near Dallas, and John Abbott, a friend, colleague and entomologist from the University of Texas at Austin, had asked one of the "wardens," locals that acted as both guides and guards, to get us down a little closer to the colony for some photos. John and Dan had been participants on one of the first trips that Tom Emmel, a lepidopterist from the University of Florida at Gainesville, had led to the Monarch's overwintering grounds and they themselves were here, in homage to Tom, leading their first trip with Pat and I and a dozen other participants along for the ride.

I don't know if I'll ever be able to convey the excitement that I felt as we cautiously made our way downslope and then back up a short ways until we were nose to branch with a tree completely covered in butterflies. I still can't recall if the shortness of breath I was having was due to the exercise I was getting (at an elevation that, frankly, I wasn't prepared for) or the sheer joy of where I was and what I was doing. As we made our way to a vantage point that would permit photos, I inadvertently brushed a butterfly-laden branch and was horrified to see many of the butterflies fall off of it like so much dandelion fluff in a stiff breeze. I thought I might cry until I remembered the "rescued" male that I had proudly resuscitated on the slopes above. Perhaps these butterflies, too, would survive my clumsiness. I tried to remind myself of just what they had already been through and that they weren't nearly as fragile as they appeared.

As we took a few photos the sun finally hit the tops of the trees above us and we were soon enveloped in what can only be described as "orange snow." Looking

The Monarch's overwintering roosts are almost exclusively found in the Oyamel forests of the Sierra Volcanica Transversal, *or Transverse Neovolcanic Range of central Mexico. At an average elevation of 2,500 m (8,200 ft), this mountain range includes some of the highest peaks in Mexico.*

Monarchs flying in a forest clearing give one the impression that orange snow is falling. Deforestation is a key issue at the Mexican overwintering roost sites. Trees buffer the butterflies from wind, rain, and extremes in temperature. Fewer trees not only mean fewer places to roost, but a weakening of the forest overall.

up we saw thousands of butterflies flying, slipping and gliding through the gaps between the trees with more being added until, finally, I thought I would stop breathing. It wasn't the irruption of butterflies that I had been told about, when the sound of millions of pairs of wings all beating together could be almost deafening, but it was awe-inspiring all the same...

Life in the Trees

Of course, Monarchs do not know, nor much care I imagine, that we find their sojourns in the mountains of central Mexico so magical. The interesting thing is that they're here at all, and in such large numbers.

All of the overwintering roosts or colonies in the states of Michoacan and Mexico are between 70 and 170 km (44–105 mi) west of Mexico City in the Oyamel Fir (*Abies religiosa*, Pinaceae) forests of Mexico's Transverse Neovolcanic Range that lie between 18° and 19°N latitude. At an average elevation of 2,500 m (8,200 ft), but reaching over 3,650 m (12,000 ft) on some peaks, this mountain range includes some of the highest peaks in Mexico. The Oyamel forests, which are preferred almost exclusively by the butterflies, occur in 13 "islands" of vegetation on some of the tallest peaks. Nine of these vegetation islands, which are, ecologically speaking, relict boreal forests which persist at this altitude, occur within the *Sierra Volcanica Transversal*. Five of the ranges within this belt of mountains, covering an area of only 800 sq km (309 sq mi)— the Sierra Campanario, Sierra Chincua, Sierra Chivati, Sierra Pelon and Sierra Picacho—usually have one or more of the overwintering roosts each year.

The Oyamel forests are critical habitat for the overwintering Monarchs. During the summer, when the butterflies are not in residence, these forests are characteristically "cloud forests," damp with fog for much of the day. They harbor a rich herbaceous understory that is somewhat unusual for a "boreal" forest. During the winter the forests provide the conditions necessary to the overwintering butterflies, including moderately cold temperatures that promote torpor but are not lethal, warming during the day to allow activity (but not too much excessively energy-draining activity), and enough humidity to prevent fires and desiccation of the butterflies.

Temperatures under the firs have been shown to be 2° to 5°C (4°–9°F) warmer than in nearby clearings and moderate thinning of the forest canopy

Oyamel Fir (Abies religiosa) *forests are critical habitat for the overwintering Monarchs in Mexico. During the winter the trees moderate cold temperatures to promote torpor without being lethal, and provide enough humidity to prevent fires and desiccation. The rich herbaceous understory of the forests also harbors a wealth of winter wildflowers that provide needed nectar resources.*

"Look out for the butterflies!" Forest clearing and increasing tourism continue to encroach on the Monarch's overwintering sites despite the Mexican government's early decree to set aside some 16,000 hectares (40,000 acres) as protected areas.

can reduce the temperature by as much as 2°C (4°F). The temperature buffering ability of the Oyamel forest is excellent with normal ranges being confined to minimums of 6° to 9° C (42°–48°F) and maximums of 13° to 15°C (56°–60°F), a total range of only 4° to 9°C (8°–18°F). The forest understory also has a wealth of winter wildflowers that provide nectar and the valley bottoms contain streams where the butterflies may drink. The slopes of the mountains also allow the roosts to move up or down the slope in concert with the prevailing temperature regimes: roosts often form up high in the early winter but are found further down the slopes by the time winter temperatures drop to dangerous levels.

Trouble in Paradise

The sheer magnitude and incredible scope of its annual autumnal migration have earmarked the Monarch as the poster child of an entirely new class of endangerment, the "endangered phenomenon," and much has been written in this context of the conservation issues at the overwintering roosts. While I

Butterflies or leaves? Monarchs will stay in their overwintering roosts for four or five months, and for much of that time many may not move at all, other than to jockey for position among the crowded branches.

believe that conservation issues are just as real and of considerable concern throughout the rest of the Monarch's range, I don't wish to downplay issues at the overwintering roosts, so I will dwell on them briefly here.

Without doubt the most critical problems faced in the overwintering roosts are habitat damage and loss. It wasn't until 1976 that the world learned the answer to the riddle of where all those Monarchs went through the disclosure of the general location of overwintering roosts in *National Geographic*. It's important to realize that even then, habitat degradation and loss through forest clearing and tree removal were ongoing problems. These issues prompted many concerned and interested people to lobby the Mexican government for protective legislation. In

ROOST SIZES AND CONSERVATION

Accurately estimating the population size of the half dozen or so main Monarch colonies—more than 30 sites have been identified but occupancy varies substantially among colonies and from year to year—is, as might be expected, difficult. Bill Calvert of Texas Monarch Watch has used two methods—common mark-release-recapture methods and forest parameters such as tree and branch size, density, and counts of butterflies per unit area—and both methods have suggested that there were approximately 13 million butterflies per hectare (about 6 million butterflies per acre). More recently, random samples of dead butterflies on the forest floor after major winter storms have suggested that the density of butterflies varies a great deal between sites but may be as many as 20 to 70 million butterflies per hectare (about 9–32 million butterflies per acre).

The amount of forest cover estimated to be used by Monarchs declined significantly from 7.8 ha (17 acres) in the winter of 1994–95 to 2.3 ha (5 acres) in 2000–01. Using Dr. Calvert's estimate of 13 million butterflies per hectare, this suggests that the total number of butterflies at the roosting sites declined from more than 100 million to only 30 million during this period. However, large year-to-year fluctuations in Monarch numbers are common. The size of the 2001–02 colonies increased remarkably up to an estimated 9.4 ha (21 acres) and about 120 million butterflies. These large differences in the number of butterflies arriving at the Mexican overwintering roosts strongly suggest that what happens away from the roosts—during the flight north, in the breeding range and the migration south—are also of major importance in the conservation and survival of the eastern North American Monarch.

This is not to imply that conservation efforts at the overwintering roosts are not important. For example, a major winter storm in January of 2002 is estimated to have killed 63 to 73 percent of the 120 million butterflies present, leaving around 40 million butterflies to make the northward journey. This is only slightly higher than the low previous years' estimate of 30 million. As Orley "Chip" Taylor of Monarch Watch observed, it is lucky that the January 2002 storm did not occur a year earlier, when the population was already depressed. A 65 percent mortality event in 2001 would have decimated the overwintering population to leave only about 10 million butterflies to journey north.

Clearly, major climatic events at the overwintering roosts, combined with ongoing concerns such as forest clearing, general global warming and even the effects of tourism, may have a major impact on potential breeding population size. However, the fourfold increase in the numbers of butterflies arriving at the roost sites between 2000 and 2001 also shows the impact and importance of reproductive success in the breeding range.

October of 1986, the Mexican government decreed that five of the known over-wintering sites were to be protected by non-disturbance cores surrounded by buffer zones for monitoring loss and damage to the reserves. The original 16,000 ha (40,000 acres) was expanded to 56,000 ha (138,000 acres) by a further decree in November of 2000.

Forest clearing remains an acute problem. Individual Monarch butterflies can survive light freezing temperatures when conditions are relatively dry, and the Oyamel forests are thick and provide excellent forest cover to both buffer drops in temperature and protect the butterflies from precipitation and frost. Obviously, forest clearing removes trees in quantity, and the progression of forest loss in the buffer zones has reduced most of the major roost sites to their core protection zones. The resulting smaller forests have less area and more edge (leading to intrusion by predators that would not normally forage in deep forest) and allow the penetration of wind, rain and storm. Similarly, removing of individual trees within the core protective zones has opened the canopy,

Monarchs drinking on the ground. As spring approaches and the over-wintering roosts begin to break up in late February and early March, many Monarchs are nearing the end of their internal reserves and come down from the trees to forage for nectar and water.

Karen Oberhauser, a Monarch researcher from the University of Minnesota, holds male and female Monarchs to show their differences. The male (top) possess two alar pockets (dark spots) on the hind-wing that the female (below) lacks.

reduced the temperature- and moisture-buffering capabilities of the forests, and increased the forests' susceptibility to permanent damage from fire.

The real problem, of course, is the same as elsewhere: too many people, not enough employment and not enough resources. The locals depend on the forests for firewood and have been nibbling away at the forests for many years. It's not difficult to see that the conservation problems at the Monarch roosts are not just biological but also legal, sociological and monetary. Most recently, tourism and all of the economic effects that it brings has become a boon, but only to some groups. Others decry tourism as yet another pressure on the forests and the Monarchs.

Two Monarchs mate. As spring progresses, the increasing number of butterflies flying about coupled with the gradual end of reproductive diapause yields an increase in mating activity. Once a female has mated and has begun to mature her eggs, she begins to search for host plants on which to lay them.

Preparing for a Journey

The overwintering roosts begin to break up in late February and early March, although it has been suggested that roost dissolution is happening progressively earlier, possibly caused by global warming trends. Monarchs have been in the roost for four or five months now, and for much of that time some may not have moved at all, other than to jockey for position among the crowded branches. If the temperature and humidity are just so, and the butterflies have been able to conserve their lipid mass during migration and by not being metabolically active, then movement is probably not needed. Others, especially those relegated to the edges of individual groups of butterflies or those that have smaller lipid reserves, make infrequent forays into the air attempting to obtain a more protected position within the colony. But as spring approaches, many of the butterflies are nearing the end of their internal reserves and must forage for nectar and water.

Downslope flights seeking these resources are common in the late morning and afternoons of the weeks preceding roost dissolution. Visitors are often surprised to see butterflies congregated around seeps and runoffs in the lower portions of the roosting areas drinking water, since we so infrequently observe this behavior in most butterflies. In fact, many species of butterflies seek out water, often in the form of dewdrops or unevaporated raindrops on plant leaves, early in the day. Others, of course, obtain moisture indirectly through flower nectar or puddling for mineral salts in moist ground at the edges of streams, ponds and puddles. Still, the numbers of Monarchs that are often found drinking water directly during the early spring or late winter at the roosting colonies often startles many.

Surprisingly, or maybe not so surprisingly, the areas near the roosts have abundant flowers. Roosts form at the elevations that straddle the cusp between too cold and not cold enough and too wet and not humid enough, so the slopes just below the roosts are warmer and wetter and often provide just about perfect conditions for many species of wildflowers. With spring approaching, increasing number of flowers bloom, and more and more Monarchs seek them out to replenish the internal resources that they have slowly but inexorably been depleting by the simple act of staying alive through the winter. The maturation of their reproductive organs as their reproductive diapause slowly ends also uses energy.

The increasing number of butterflies flying about coupled with the gradual end of reproductive diapause yields an increase in mating activity as the season progresses. Monarch mating is unusual among butterflies, even among its closest relatives in the Danainae, as the males are quite aggressive. So aggressive, in fact, that they will frequently throw themselves at a suitable object—basically anything around that is the same size, color and shape—grapple with it while the two butterflies fall through the air until they hit the ground, and then hold on tightly while they attempt to copulate. Males seem remarkably poor at being able to identify the opposite sex, however, and frequently attack each other. Fully one-third of the mating attempts and copulations that I saw at El Rosario were male-male pairs locked in "mortal combat."

Still, enough male-female matings occur that essentially all of the females—the major proportion of which were, by definition through reproductive diapause, virgins—are mated in the days and weeks leading to the dissolution of the colonies. Once a female has mated and has begun to mature her eggs, she

Among butterflies, Monarch mating is unusually aggressive. Males in particular will frequently throw themselves at potential partners. Yet they seem remarkably poor at being able to identify the opposite sex, and frequently attack each other, as shown here.

begins to search for host plants on which to lay them. Why north? Why not just hang around central Mexico and use local milkweeds? These are *big* butterflies, and the average milkweed can only support the complete growth and development of one or two caterpillars. So where do you go when all of the local milkweeds are full? Why, you follow the sun, of course.

Guided by the sun, increasing day length and the slow, inevitable change of season, female Monarchs on the migration north arrive in Texas. The first stop on their northward journey and one of their last on the migration south, Texas is the funnel through which the entire population of migrating Monarchs must pass.

CHAPTER 3

North by Northeast

L ESS THAN A WEEK AFTER WE HAD RETURNED HOME from our trip to the Monarch sanctuaries at El Rosario and Sierra Chincua, a severe winter storm hit the Michoacan mountains. Winds estimated at over 100 km/h (62 mph) per hour drove snow and ice through the mountains, downing many trees and damaging most of the others that remained standing. Two small colonies of Monarchs at La Herrada and Cerro Pelon were decimated and the mortality rates for the relatively small numbers of butterflies there were estimated at upwards of 80 percent.

The storm was not considered to be as strong near the town of Angangueo, the base for our—and many other—expeditions to the El Rosario and Sierra Chincua colonies. Still, the Chincua colony received more than a meter of snow (over 40 in.) and had low temperatures of −8°C (18°F). El Rosario fared marginally better, with only about a tenth of the snow (nearly 10 cm or 4 in.) and temperatures only slightly below freezing (−4°C or 25°F). Mortality at the two colonies was estimated at nearly eight percent but because these are two of the most populous colonies—especially Sierra Chincua that year—the number of butterflies lost was almost as high as that at La Herrada and Cerro Pelon.

So to put this all into perspective, we visited the colonies during a year that is widely thought to have had one of the lowest roost recruitments since attempts have been made to estimate the numbers of butterflies at the colonies. And shortly after we left, a storm further reduced the population to a still lower number. Of course, this number was still in the 18 to 22 million range but this is considerably less than the beginning number from this or previous seasons. What effect would the low number of migrants have on the journey north that year? What effect would it have on the breeding population, and subsequent southward migration?

Amazingly, the low population size of northward migrants had little effect on the timing of their reappearance at their first stops in northern Mexico and Texas.

At the Stengl "Lost Pines" Biology Station near Smithville in central Texas, we generally expect to see our first Monarchs within a day or two of March 18, and March 2001 was no exception—a female was seen in the yard on March 19. By the time that Monarchs get to central Texas the population has dispersed sufficiently to make it difficult to estimate numbers, but my impression that year was that the numbers did not seem unusually small.

The first arrivals in Texas in mid-March are "primary" migrants; isolated individual butterflies that have mated at the overwintering colony (or shortly thereafter) and traveled as far north as the station. Along the way, females seek out seedlings and young milkweeds, lay an egg or two, and continue north, leaving a generation of progeny behind them to continue the journey north. Think of it as a "leap-frog" migration with the generation left behind eventually surpassing the parents in their northward trek. We don't usually see these "secondary" migrants at the "Lost Pines" until mid-April when there's a noticeable influx of bright orange, fresh adults.

We also often don't see any males until this second "wave" reaches us but sometimes we do see a number of first wave males. On March 18, 2002, for example, I watched a group of eight or so Monarchs nectaring at pear blossoms. These were just about the only thing in bloom because we had had a number of late season freezes that delayed most of the spring wildflowers. At least three of the butterflies at the tree were amorous, frustrated males that were aggressively attacking the others, knocking them out of the air and attempting to copulate on the ground.

We're lucky here in central Texas if we see Monarchs for more than about a month in the spring and the same in the fall. Not at all like what I was familiar with in southern Ontario, where they would generally arrive in late May and we could see Monarchs just about everywhere until late September or so. Still, Texas is like a funnel through which the entire population of migrating Monarchs must pass, being one of their last stops on the migration south and one of their first on the journey north…

The First Stop

It's difficult to underestimate the importance of Texas in the migration of the Monarch butterfly, regardless of whether you are considering the flight north in the Spring or the migration south in the Fall. Texas is the first stop north and

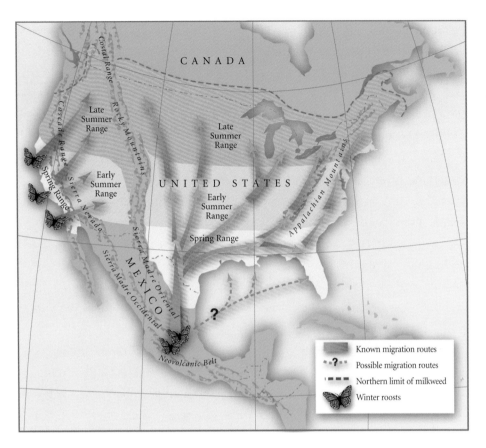

Each spring, millions of Monarchs depart their overwintering roosts in Mexico, embarking on a long journey north. Following the gradual availability of milkweeds as spring advances from south to north, the Monarchs migrate in leap-frog fashion, with each successive generation eventually surpassing the parents in their northward trek.

the last stop south. What effect do conditions in Texas have on the population of females that are flying north in the spring?

Guided by the sun, increasing day length and the slow, inevitable change of season, females painstakingly seek out suitable milkweeds on which to lay their eggs. The problem is that at this time of year these are plants that are in many cases barely out of the ground. I've tried to find milkweed seedlings and sprouts as late as mid-April in central Texas and can readily attest to the painstaking part. Luckily, the butterflies are much better at this task. It's fascinating to watch a female Monarch cruising low over the meadows and fields, alighting every now and then to test the foliage of some potential sprout or another.

The availability of host plant sprouts at this time of year assumes that it has been a "good" year. If there has been sufficient winter rainfall, if the winter hasn't been cold, with long, hard freezes, and there have been few (if any) late season freezes—and if the milkweeds had the time, rainfall and nutrient resources in the previous growing season to complete their growth or set seed—

The first Monarch arrivals in central Texas in mid-March are "primary" migrants, butterflies that have lived for as much as eight months, have mated at the overwintering sites, and flown a further 1,200 km (750 mi) north. A month later, a second generation of butterflies arrive, from the eggs the females laid along the way.

MILKWEEDS AND MIGRATION

As we have seen, the Danainae butterflies, of which the Monarch is a member, are primarily tropical and subtropical in origin. Not too surprisingly, the plant family Asclepiadaceae—including the milkweed host plants of the Monarch, members of the genus *Asclepias*—are similarly tropical and subtropical in origin. Concordance in the worldwide distribution of these two groups is expected and, of course, the Monarch wouldn't travel to and from higher latitudes if there were not temperate members of the Asclepiads. So the question "Why does the eastern North American Monarch migrate from lower to higher latitudes, then return each winter?" could easily be reconsidered as "Why are there temperate members of the milkweed family?"

The milkweed family is much larger and far more extensive than the number of butterfly taxa that use it as host plants. There are nearly 350 genera containing some 3,000 species of these herbs, shrubs, twining lianas and (rarely) trees, around the tropics. The large number of species and genera is a good indication that the Asclepiadaceae is a very successful plant family within suitable habitat. If we examine the temperate species, we find that less than 5 percent of the family is found outside of the tropics. In other words, Asclepiads had no need to colonize temperate regions to be successful. So, why bother? Well, because they can—there's more than a little truth to the old adage that "nature abhors a vacuum."

The fact that milkweeds occur outside of the tropics, together with the fact that they are seasonal and require fairly specific conditions in which to grow (because they have adapted from tropical ancestors) and the Danaine's predilection for migration go a long way to explaining the reach of Monarch migration and continental recoloniza-

then there will be milkweed sprouts for females to find and lay eggs on. But if any of these conditions haven't been met, or if the butterflies leave the roosts earlier than they should, then they could arrive before there are plants available for their eggs. This is exactly what may have happened in Texas in 1995 and 1996, then again in 1998 and 2000.

Droughts can have drastic effects on plant survival and their availability, not just on suitable milkweed host plants, but on the flowers and nutrient sources that are needed to sustain Monarch flight and life as well. Even if there are barely adequate nectar resources, droughts reduce the growth of milkweeds so that there are fewer leaves and smaller plants that may not be able to support the complete development of caterpillars. Leaf quality of drought-stressed plants also declines so those caterpillars grow more slowly and are more susceptible to disease and fungal pathogens, and to predation.

tion. In fact, if it weren't for a few wildly successful temperate milkweeds, it's very likely that the Monarch's phenomenal migration would be a great deal smaller and far less spectacular. Of the more than 100 species of Asclepias that occur in North America, only a half dozen or so are responsible for the extent of the northward expansion of the Monarch range that we know today.

The diversity of milkweeds declines as one moves north, from some 60 species in Mexico, to 30 species in Texas, a little more than 20 species in Kansas, around a dozen in Ohio and Southern Ontario, to only one or two around 50°N latitude and the states and provinces along the Atlantic seaboard. The "center" of Monarch summer breeding range—where more than 50 percent of Monarchs at the overwintering roosts originate from—is in the so-called "Corn Belt." At this latitude and position there are an average of around 14 milkweed species available for the Monarch.

Outside of the Corn Belt region the number of available milkweed species drops quickly to an average of less than five, with the most common species being *Asclepias speciosa*, *A. syriaca*, *A. incarnata*, and *A. tuberosa*. Early cardenolide "fingerprinting," which determined that Monarchs retained the chemical defenses of their host plants in direct correlation with that of the milkweeds that they fed on as caterpillars, showed that the vast majority of butterflies at the roosts—about 85 percent—had fed on *A. syriaca*, the common milkweed, or *A. speciosa*, the showy milkweed, species that only occur north of about 37°N latitude. Interestingly, Monarchs that feed on these two species, which are known to possess poor quality cardenolides, have the lowest concentration of cardenolides and are more likely to be preyed upon at the winter roosts.

Predators are legion, and Monarch eggs and growing caterpillars must contend with all manner of invertebrate and vertebrate predators anywhere in their range. But Texas also has a super-predator: fire ants. The imported alien fire ant, *Solenopsis invicta* (Hymenoptera), rather than the native *S. geminata*, is a major threat. Where this invasive species from South America is found the diversity of all terrestrial life, vertebrates as well as insects, spiders and other invertebrates, is greatly depressed.

You might be thinking, "aren't Monarch caterpillars protected by the noxious chemicals, the cardenolides, that they sequester from the milkweeds?" Unfortunately, as effective as these defenses can be against vertebrate predators, they seem to have little to no effect on many insect and spider predators. Fire ants are voracious predators of moth and butterfly caterpillars and controlled studies by Bill Calvert of Texas Monarch Watch have shown nearly 100 percent

Often despised as unattractive weeds with toxic leaves and sap, milkweeds (genus Asclepias*) are the Monarch's sole caterpillar food plants and are key to its survival and reproduction. The Monarch depends on only a small number of the more than 100 species of milkweeds found in North America. Shown, clockwise from top left: common milkweed (*Asclepias syriaca*), swamp milkweed (*A. incarnata*), showy milkweed (*A. speciosa*), and butterfly milkweed or butterflyweed (*A. tuberosa*).*

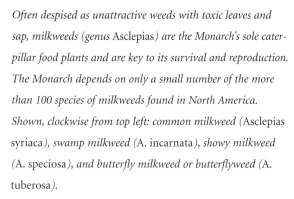

mortality of early stages wherever fire ants are present. Even where fire ant numbers are low (even the omnivorous fire ant is affected by drought conditions), Monarch egg and caterpillar survival is a long shot at best.

Still, in "average" years—although my friend and colleague, Larry Gilbert, a native Texan, is quick to point out that "average" in Texas is an anomaly—Monarchs do manage to replace themselves in enough numbers to continue their journey north by northeast. While the imported fire ant is thus far a southern problem, similar perils—weather conditions that modify plant growth, germination and reproduction or flowering, or cycling of predator populations in tandem with other factors—are encountered all along the journey north and throughout the eventual breeding range. Monarchs, like most other organisms, are at the mercy of the elements.

Continuity

Whichever way you look at it, Monarchs, like most other butterflies, face remarkable odds in their early stages, often approaching or exceeding 99 percent against them. Let's take a hypothetical case where a typical female Monarch is capable of producing and laying 500 eggs in her reproductive lifetime. This is reasonably close to the known lifetime fecundity of the 400 to 500 eggs that wild females with full life spans can lay. At a one percent survival rate, this would mean that only five of those eggs survive to become butterflies themselves. (In the real world, this is overly optimistic; in fact, many species of butterfly are lucky if they manage to have *one* of their progeny survive to replace them.)

A 5:1 replacement rate is actually pretty good. If half of 20 million northward migrating Monarchs are female, and half of those survive as far as Texas and even half of them have managed to lay all of the eggs that they are capable of laying then those 2.5 million females will generate 12.5 million progeny. This doesn't include the partially successful females that, say, average one replacement for every 100 eggs but don't survive long enough to complete their laying or those that have only been able to lay partial egg loads along the way to Texas because host plants are scarce. So it's not inconceivable that the 10 million females that began the journey could generate as many as 30 million progeny or so. Carry this through the next couple of generations and you can see that the next generation's 15 million females (one-half of 30 million progeny) may

BOOM AND BUST

Reliable estimates have established the Mexican Monarch population of fall 2001 around 120 million or so butterflies, four times higher than it was in fall 2000. This was a stark reversal of the declines in previous years; there were an estimated 110 million Monarchs in the fall of 1999 but only 30 million in the fall of 2000. In other words, instead of the possible 5:1 replacement rate seen in 2001 there was probably much less than a 1:1 replacement rate, possibly as low as 1:4 in 2000.

So what was different between the breeding seasons of 2000, when numbers declined drastically, and 2001, when the population size increased by some 500 percent? First and foremost, and potentially key, was the occurrence of a winter/spring drought in Texas that left Monarchs struggling to find enough flowers to maintain flight or host plants to lay eggs on before their conserved energy was depleted. (Remember, these are six- to eight-month-old butterflies that migrated all the way down to Mexico in the fall of 1999.) Worse, the drought in 2000 was not confined to Texas but was more widespread, throughout the southern portion of their normal breeding range.

This by itself would be enough to cause a significant decline in the first two generations, however, "good" conditions in the northern part of the breeding range could allow for a decent

recovery that compensated for the loss due to southern droughts. In 2000, however, much of the northeast was plagued by cool, wet conditions that helped to prevent females from laying all of their eggs (if cool, wet weather prevents you from flying then you can't find plants on which to lay eggs). Eggs and early instar caterpillars may also have succumbed to fungus problems or pathogens while later caterpillar development would be slowed by the cool temperatures. The slower the caterpillar growth then the longer they are on the plants and available to caterpillar-hunting predators. Cool and wet can be just as damaging as hot and dry.

So, 2000 was a bust all the way around—drought affecting the returning migrants and the first generation in the south, and the opposite problem, wet and cool conditions, affecting the reproductive success of the second through fourth generations in the north. That year there were still caterpillars on milkweeds in late September and early October long after the migration south would have been well underway. But 2001 was a boom year with near to perfect conditions throughout the range. These two years, alone, provide a wonderful and useful illustration of the effects that environmental conditions during the northward recolonization phase can have on the size of the overwintering population in Mexico.

generate 45 million progeny, then 25 million or so females can yield 75 million butterflies, and so on. This scenario, given more than a little license in the variation between locations and generations, is possibly quite similar to what actually happened in 2001 (*See "Boom and Bust" above*).

A Monarch caterpillar feeds on a milkweed plant. To avoid the latex sap, which can gum up the mandibles of the caterpillar, Monarch caterpillars frequently "notch" the main veins of the leaves to stop the flow of latex through them. Like the Monarch, milkweeds are tropical in origin and only a relatively few species that have adapted to temperate conditions are responsible for the northward expansion of the Monarch's range, and their subsequent phenomenal migrations south.

Availability of host plants on the migration path north plays a crucial role in the succeeding generation of Monarchs. If milkweeds did not get the time, rainfall and nutrient resources to complete their growth in the previous growing season, or if butterflies arrive too early, there will be fewer milkweed sprouts for females to find and lay eggs on. Here a Monarch caterpillar nourishes itself on a tropical milkweed on its journey northward.

Journey's End

The end of the journey for a northward-migrating Monarch depends on which generation is undertaking the journey. The primary migrants do not, as a general rule, return much further north than Texas, although there are records of primary migrants presumed to have flown as far north as upstate New York. The majority of the secondary migrants from the generation that develops in northern Mexico and Texas will end their journey in the mid-eastern states or the southern Corn Belt states. In turn, the tertiary migrants from the second generation will journey further north and complete much of the recolonization of their range. This means that, depending on where you live in northeastern North America, you may not see Monarchs until as late as the end of May and beginning of June.

This is about the time that we were used to seeing our first Monarchs of the year in the Toronto area on the north shore of Lake Ontario. Monarchs really don't venture very far into Canada. Through most of the prairie provinces and western Ontario, the distribution of milkweed, and thus the distribution of breeding Monarchs, ends at around 50° to 52°N latitude, just a bit further north of the U.S.-Canada border at the 49th Parallel. Of course, central and southwestern Ontario is a different story since it reaches down to around 41°N latitude (Point Pelee, the southern tip of Ontario, is actually at the same latitude as the north border of the state of California).

The distributional limit of milkweeds and the potential breeding grounds of the Monarch in Ontario extend eastward from the line across the prairies up around the north and east shore of Lake Superior, along the northern shore of Lake Huron to Sudbury, North Bay and Highway 17 east to the Ottawa region. In eastern Canada, milkweed range limits include the southern and western parts of Nova Scotia, New Brunswick and the Gaspé region of the south shore of Quebec, crossing the St. Lawrence just northeast of Quebec City and continuing southwest towards Ottawa. Through much of this range there is only one or at most two species of milkweed, a far cry from the 30-some species that are known in Texas, or the nearly 60 species in Mexico. Ontario, with a total of 11 species, is the central portion of the Monarch's eastern range in Canada.

Monarchs sometimes overshoot the range limits of milkweeds and there are records from as far north as the Hudson and James Bay lowlands, through the prairies up to about 56°N latitude, and even a record or two from the Northwest Territories north of Alberta and into northern British Columbia. Similarly, there

A northwest migrant refuels at flowers in south-central Texas. Droughts can have drastic effects not only on the availability of milkweed host plants but on the flowers and nutrient sources that are needed to sustain Monarch's flight.

49

A Monarch caterpillar feeds on a milkweed plant. Like the Monarch, the milkweed is tropical in origin, although of the more than 100 species of milkweed that occur in North America, only a half dozen or so are responsible for the phenomenal migration of the Monarch and the northward expansion of its range.

The end of the journey for spring migrants varies with the generation but some reach distances of more than 4,500 km (2,800 mi) from their winter roosts in Mexico. Here a male Monarch nectars at tansy (Tanacetum vulgare, Compositae) near North Bay, Ontario, a distance of 3,700 km (2,300 miles) north of Mexico."

are almost yearly records of Monarchs being found in Newfoundland, although there are no native milkweeds on that island. Strictly speaking, Monarchs are not limited to the range limits of milkweed but they are not capable of reproducing beyond the limits of their obligate larval host plants.

So, depending on where you live in eastern North America, you may see primary returning migrants or the first, second or even third generation of Monarchs on their northward journey. And while people in Texas and the south might only see Monarchs during the two migration periods in the Spring and the Fall, folks in the north will see them pretty consistently for up to four months. During this time they will have two to three generations, each lasting for up to two months (about one month as egg, caterpillar and pupa, and up to one month as a butterfly), before the final generation once again turns its sights southward to Mexico.

Summer in North America seems idyllic for the Monarch, seen here in a field of goldenrods. Yet the Monarch's northern breeding grounds is no bed of roses, and is also home to a variety of predators, parasites and pathogens, from birds to vines, ants to humans, herbicides to genetically-engineered corn.

CHAPTER 4

Living in America

t was my first stark, bitter realization of our environmental carelessness. It had only been eight years since I last visited the north-eastern corner of the Charles Sauriol Conservation Reserve in Toronto's East Don River Valley. I recalled this little valley—part of what is often called "a rare patch of urban wilderness"—as a wondrous butterfly-filled meadow, but it was now almost unrecognizable. What had once been a thriving, diverse eco-system that sustained more than 35 or so species of butterflies was now choking, overflowing with an alien invader, the aptly named "dog-strangling vine" or black swallowwort, Vincetoxicum (Cynanchum) nigrum (Asclepiadaceae). That a place could change so much in so little time genuinely startled me.

My first visit to this spot was in the early summer of 1986. I had been system-atically exploring the many access points into the Don Valley park system, doing some birding and butterflying before heading to work, when I "discovered" this little oasis, a meadow along the east bank of the East Don. It was alive with but-terflies and I was intoxicated by the variety and abundance I stumbled into—I knew I was going to be late for work!

I remember watching Monarchs gliding among the milkweeds and seeing large numbers of at least a half-dozen species of hairstreaks, as many kinds of skippers, including the large silver-spotted skipper, both common and orange sulphurs and more tiger swallowtails than I think I had ever seen before, jockeying for positions on the blooms. I was thrilled to discover some turtleheads attended by Baltimore checkerspots along the bank of the river and pearly eyes along the edge of the woods. There were more kinds of wildflowers than I could count and every one seemed to have a butterfly, beetle or bee busily foraging on it.

This diversity—and my wonder at it—was one of those experiences that gal-vanized and reinforced my decision to return to school, to study the biology of plant and insect interactions, and devote the rest of my life to doing what I truly enjoyed.

After having finished my undergraduate degree and more than halfway through my doctoral studies, I returned to this spot on a Toronto Entomologists' Association butterfly count in 1994. It was an eye-opener, to say the least.

The plant and butterfly diversity was less than half of what it had been eight years previously. Eight experienced counters encountered only seventeen species of butterflies with only single individuals of seven of those species—including only a single Monarch—being seen. Only a single individual of one of the half-dozen hairstreak species that I had marveled at in 1986 were still present and the milkweed they had been nectaring on had almost completely vanished under a carpet of swallowwort.

Appropriate to its name, the swallowwort had taken over and had nearly swallowed the entire meadow whole. The only region that still had some remnant of the previous diversity was along the very verges of the river. There, there were still some turtleheads with two or three Baltimores flitting amongst them but the pearly eyes along the boundary between the meadow and the woods had vanished, as had the sulphurs, the tiger swallowtails and most of the skippers.

In their places were hundreds of grass-feeding European skippers, Thymelicus lineola *(Hesperiidae)—an invader that competes with the native skippers—tame bees, one or two species of beetles and the stark monoculture of the clonal swallowwort. The destruction was almost total. If I hadn't already known this very meadow I would have doubted that there had ever been abundant life here. It reminded me uncannily of what purple loosestrife,* Lythrum salicaria *(Lythraceae), did to the marshes of the northeast (and is currently doing to much of the northwest)—move in, multiply and force everything else out.*

It was not a pretty picture.

Trials and Tribulations

The main breeding grounds of the Monarch butterfly, that area north of about 38° or 39°N latitude up to the limits of milkweed range in Canada, is no bed of roses. My main thesis throughout this book has been that the conservation issues, problems, trials and tribulations that face the eastern North American Monarch population in their breeding grounds and along their migration routes are just as pervasive, just as endangering, and just as consequential as those that they face in their Mexican overwintering sites. What are these issues

Naïve birds, after tasting their first Monarch, seldom attack again. Here a Monarch nectaring at flowers shows the kind of damage to its left hindwing that results from a bird attack. A single "taste" of the noxious compounds in the wing scales that are left from caterpillar feeding on milkweeds is enough to deter most birds.

and how do they impact Monarch breeding, survival, migration and population dynamics? Is "living in America"—or perhaps more appropriately "dying in America"—an accurate description of the future of the Monarch butterfly in eastern North America?

Foremost among the issues facing the Monarch throughout its breeding range and migratory pathways—not unlike the overwintering sites—is habitat degradation, fragmentation and outright loss. Much of the breeding range and the areas traveled over during migration are the most populous parts of the continent. Surprisingly, habitat changes due to human land use modifications can at times be beneficial. For example, forest clearing for agricultural use in central Ontario between 1940 and 1990 produced a significant northward increase in the range of the common milkweed (*Asclepias syriaca*), from 43° to 47°N latitude, and a concomitant increase in the occurrence of the Monarch.

However, the majority of anthropogenic changes in land use and continuity have resulted in major losses of Monarch habitat. Other threats include the many environmental changes that accompany our "progress"; the myriad other forms of competition that occur between butterflies and humankind; changes to the natural balance of communities through the introduction of invasive, alien species; the wholesale spraying of pesticides and herbicides; and our failure to regulate, legislate or otherwise control our own activities.

Environmental Concerns

It is too early to know for sure, but global warming probably already impacts, or will soon impact, Monarch populations. We already know from research conducted on other species in both North America and Europe that butterfly ranges are expanding northward and contracting northward along their former southern edges. The ranges of entire species have been shown to have shifted up to 240 km (150 mi) north in a relatively short time (less than a century) and with a relatively small global temperature increase (estimated to be approximately 0.8°C or 1.5°F). The majority of climatologists and biogeographers predict that the rate of temperature change will likely double, up to 1.5°C (3°F), in less than one-half the time (within the next 50 years). Most agree that the consequences of this seemingly minor change to the distributions and population dynamics of plants and animals will be devastating.

What is most interesting when contemplating what global warming might mean to the Monarch is that the effects will almost certainly be negative at the overwintering roosts and potentially benign (or, in the long term negative) over the breeding range. The problem at the roosts is that the butterflies overwinter on mountain slopes, and mountains have finite heights—there is only so far you can move up a mountain slope before you reach the top and have nowhere else to go. Where will Monarchs roost if the mountains are not high enough to support the boreal community that might buffer the coming temperature change? There are already indications that the butterflies may be leaving the roost sites earlier than they once were, possibly a response to changes in seasonality already brought about by climatic warming.

At the other end of the range the consequences are less certain. It is probable that increasing temperatures will allow the current distributional limits of

milkweeds to shift northwards, while, at the same time, the southern limits will likely contract as conditions become less tenable. The net result of this shift could be neutral to the Monarch if agricultural land is cleared in the current northern forests at the same rate as the milkweed range moves northward, however, if there is a loss in available arable land the number of milkweeds and Monarchs could decline. Past changes in land use have generated an increase in range, likely with a similar increase in population size, but if this occurs again the larger potential population size may simply end up putting further pressure on the potentially reduced overwintering sites.

We have undoubtedly already seen harbingers of this last scenario in the past decade as a result of climatic changes triggered by El Niño and La Niña. These events, consequences of changes in the temperature of the Pacific Ocean

Butterfly gardens are patches of urban habitat for Monarchs. While they must compete with human civilization for living space, and the few remaining patches of urban wilderness are dwindling, we can supplement those losses by providing needed habitat and resources for butter-flies and other insects.

due to sinking or rising cold or warm waters, have an untoward influence on upper air currents and the path of moisture-laden air borne on the westerly winds. Seemingly minor water temperature changes have generated major climatic shifts that alternately bring drought or cool, wet conditions to the south—having a drastic effect on Texas vegetation at critical times—or to the north. These events have already produced at least fivefold fluctuations in Monarch population size from year to year.

Monarch biologists are also interested in the effects that climatic variation and changes have on caterpillar growth and development, the length of flight seasons and the number of generations that occur at different locations, as well as their effects on adult butterfly lifespan, energetics, habitat choice, nectar and host plant resource availability, and reproductive success. We just don't know enough about these subjects to be able to accurately predict the outcome. What effect do unpredictable events such as storms and heavy rainfall have on population structure and dynamics? How do fluctuations in annual patterns of rainfall and sunshine affect host plant and nectar source availability and distribution? These are just some of the questions for which we do not have adequate answers. We still have a lot of work to do.

Competition with Us

Habitat fragmentation, degradation and loss are our fault. Very few organisms are able to change the environment that they live in. To be sure, there are beavers, elephants and a few others, but none of them has nearly as much of an impact on their surroundings as *Homo sapiens* does. Seemingly innocuous activities, pursuits that we take as normal, like traveling on highways, the new subdivision being built just down the block, the use and diversion of water for our kitchens, and reclamation of a bit of wetland here and there all add up to surprising consequences. One of my students once did a project on the cumulative effect of "minor zoning variance" petitions, which in a reasonably large metropolitan area individually amounted to no more than a few meters for every request, and the total loss of green space added up to at least a hundred hectares every year.

Highways are an interesting example of the staggering yet little realized effect that we have on wildlife. Anyone with more than a casual interest in butterflies—or indeed any other kind of insect or animal—knows that vehicular traffic kills some individuals. We're used to seeing dead skunks or raccoons along the side of the road. A recent study of the magnitude of the effect of such "road kills" on moths and butterflies along public roadways in the state of Illinois, however, opened a lot of eyes. The study revealed that the number of moths and butterflies killed along the 222,000 km (138,000 mi) of highways, toll roads, county, municipal and other roads in the state probably exceeded 20 million individuals per week. The cumulative mortality of Monarchs alone was estimated to be more than 500,000 individuals. This disturbing total is between one-fortieth and one-fiftieth of the entire population of butterflies that left the Mexican roosts in 2001 and 2002. Multiply this by the number of states and kilometers of roads that Monarchs have to cross, and this source of mortality alone may account for *millions* of deaths.

Over and above highways and the steadily increasing number of bigger and bigger vehicles that use them, we compete with nature on so many levels and in so many ways that it staggers the imagination. We build, expand, channel, convert and otherwise control nature to an incredible degree—now our actions are even changing climate and weather patterns. But these are the obvious ways that we compete with wildlife. It's the unthought, unremarked and unrealized that are so insidious but damage habitats in ways that we barely recognize while it's happening. It hasn't been that long since Rachel Carson's *Silent Spring* and I think that we have yet to prove that we've actually learned anything.

Consider the effect of introduced, invasive, alien organisms such as black swallowwort (*See "Swallowwort: An Alien Invader" on page 60*), and the restriction of Monarchs to milkweed hosts. The latter has been a cause of concern due to historical trends in weed control. For example, *Asclepias syriaca*, the common milkweed, is a very successful weed that grows well in a wide variety of agricultural and non-agricultural situations. For years, economic fears of reduced yields in field crops and misplaced fears of livestock being poisoned by the toxic chemistry of milkweeds have fueled many a noxious weed list and the wide propagation of weed control legislation that encouraged the wholesale destruction of plants wherever they occurred.

Of course, the fears of farmers and ranchers have little or no basis in fact: innovations in harvesting techniques over time have made potential yield issues inconsequential and I have yet to find an unequivocal case of livestock death from consumption of milkweeds. Anyone who has seen milkweed in pastures knows that livestock avoid the plants like the plague and that milkweeds are usually the tallest and most conspicuous plants in the entire field.

SWALLOWWORT: AN ALIEN INVADER

The black swallowwort or "dog-strangling" vine, *Vincetoxicum (Cynanchum) nigrum* (Asclepiadaceae), was intentionally imported from Europe and cultivated by the Canadian and United States governments during the Second World War as a potential source of latex, when the acquisition of rubber from the usual South American sources was interrupted by enemy activity along both coasts of North America. The war effort needed rubber for tires, gaskets, grommets and washers, rubber that was in short supply, so potential alternative sources —including native species of *Asclepias*—were investigated. Needless to say, however, swallowwort escaped from cultivation and began to do what comes naturally to a vine: grow, reproduce, grow and reproduce some more.

The problem was black swallowwort was an invasive species, and in its new habitat it was able to grow and reproduce in the absence of all of the other species—herbivores, pathogens and competing plant species—that controlled the growth and size of the population in its native environment. We quickly learned that not only was black swallowwort (and native milkweeds for that matter) a poor, expensive source of latex for rubber production but it also grew rapidly, readily clambering up and over other plants—as vines are wont to do— and successfully reproduced both sexually (seed produced from flowers) and asexually (new shoots generated via underground root expansion). In fact, it reproduces by underground runners so well that it quickly forms "monoclonal" (a large number of plants all with the same genetic makeup) stands that choke, shade and kill competing plant species. Soon there's nothing left but swallowwort.

Particularly damaging for the Monarch is that black swallowwort is a member of the same plant family as milkweeds. It was feared that female Monarchs would mistake the plant for milkweeds and either lay enough eggs on the plant to reduce the number laid on their natural hosts or that the plant would prove to be incompatible with the normal development of their caterpillars. Two recent studies have allayed those fears somewhat, revealing that when given a choice between their usual milkweed and swallowwort (or, subsequently, no choice but swallowwort), females will overwhelmingly choose to lay on milkweed. The studies also confirmed that virtually none of the eggs that were laid on the swallowwort were able to complete development.

Potential problems with these studies, unfortunately, included that neither group controlled for the position of the plant in the test cages. For example, if the testing arenas were always set up so that the milkweed was always on the sunny side of the cage, is the plant or the direction of the sun responsible for the number of eggs on the plant? Similarly, neither group ever tested females only on swallowwort before they encountered a milkweed. In both studies, the researchers tested females on swallowwort alone only after exposing them to both the swallowwort and milkweed together for 48 hours. The question remains that if females are unable to find milkweeds would they accept swallowwort more readily? I actually doubt that this will make a difference to female host choice.

Intentionally imported from Europe during World War II as a potential source of latex, black swallowwort or "dog-strangling" vine, Vincetoxicum nigrum (Asclepiadaceae) quickly escaped from cultivation and has run riot in the wild, forming monoclonal stands that choke, shade and kill competing plant species— including milkweeds.

Yet being tall and conspicuous is not necessarily a virtue. Roadside and right-of-way mowing, most often for "beautification" but also sometimes for safety concerns, is another way in which we directly impact Monarchs, and other herbivorous insects and butterflies, without really thinking about it. The problem here, obviously, is the timing of mowing but it is also compounded by the simple fact that many roadside milkweeds tend to be tall, robust plants. Aesthetically they stick out like a sore thumb, often growing in relatively thick colonies of tall plants that may block sight lines and pose safety problems. Still, minimal maintenance regimes where only the very edges of the roads would be cut for safety reasons and timing mowing to coincide with natural interruptions of the developmental schedule of Monarchs would go a long way to reducing the impact of these practices.

Predators, Parasites and Pathogens

The variety of predators that target and consume butterflies is reasonably well known. Vertebrate predators include birds, lizards, snakes and a number of small rodents while invertebrate predators include spiders, dragonflies, ants, wasps and a number of predatory bugs and beetles. Unfortunately, surprisingly little is known about the specific predators of Monarchs. We do know that naïve birds, after tasting their first Monarch, will not attack one again, however, we also know that some birds at the overwintering roosts are habitual major predators of the resting butterflies. The Mexican birds bypass the noxious compounds in the butterflies by eating only those portions that have the lowest concentrations of the chemicals (which still kills the butterfly) or feeding *ad libidum* on Monarchs for a few days and then "purging" on other prey.

Lizards and snakes, while superb tropical and subtropical predators of a wide variety of butterflies and their caterpillars, are relatively scarce from the breeding range of the Monarch and are not likely to be a threat in North America. Rodents, particularly mice, shrews and voles, however, are another story. Has it occurred to you to wonder why Monarchs don't roost on the ground? After all, the ground retains daily heat better than the foliage of a tree. It's likely that the primary reason why Monarchs don't roost or rest on the ground is predation by rodents that could decimate an entire roost while the butterflies are too cold or otherwise unable to escape. Rodents are also major predators at the wintering grounds and of other roosting species of Danaines in the tropics.

One of the obstacles Monarchs face in North America is competition for
their food. The Red Milkweed Beetle (Tetraopes tetraophthalmus,
above) is one of several insect species that also feed on milkweed plants.

A large number and variety of invertebrate predators such as ants,
wasps and beetles are likely to prey on the early stages of Monarchs.
Here a second instar caterpillar is attacked by an assassin bug (Zelus
sp., Reduviidae).

Relatively few invertebrate predators are capable of preying on large adult Monarch butterflies. Some of the larger dragonflies and many orb-weaving spiders will opportunistically consume them but others will ignore them or, in the case of some web-building spiders, cut them out of the web without eating them. It's also relatively common to find smaller insects, like assassin bugs, robber flies and others, with butterfly prey. Some of these insects and spiders may be sensitive to the cardenolides in the butterfly body while others may not (although the hunger state of the predator may have a great bearing on any decision to consume caught prey).

Vertebrate predators can and do feed on the immature stages (eggs, caterpillars and pupae) of butterflies, however, the large number and variety of potential invertebrate predators are far more likely to play significant roles in the early stage mortality of Monarchs. Ants, for example, will readily consume eggs and small caterpillars but will also attack, *en masse*, larger caterpillars and chrysalids. Even predacious mites and very small insects will devour eggs. Wasps and predatory beetles and bugs are very successful at killing caterpillars whenever they encounter them. The majority of these are opportunistic predators that kill and eat whatever they find but some, like the wasps and beetles known as "caterpillar hunters," intentionally seek out and target moth and butterfly caterpillars. However, on the whole, we know disappointingly little about specific invertebrate predators of Monarchs.

Of course, predation is not the only source of potential mortality in immature Monarchs. There are also a number of parasites and parasitoids (parasitoids are parasites that usually kill their host) that will attack any insect discovered. Some will only attack moths and butterflies while still others are specific to individual species or even life history stages of specific species. Many parasitoids are small insects (often flies or wasps) that target and lay their eggs in eggs, caterpillars or pupae of a host species. The growth and development of the immature parasitoids eventually kills the host.

One of the most important and best studied parasites of Monarchs is the Neogregarine protozoan parasite *Ophryocystis elektroscirrha*. This parasite infects dermal and reproductive tissues of Monarch and Queen butterflies and is transmitted via spores that drop off an infected female while she lays eggs or are laid along with an egg. When the egg hatches the young caterpillar ingests the spores on the leaf and egg surface and is thereafter infected with the parasite. Unlike a parasitoid, *O. elektroscirrha*, does not generally kill any stage of the Monarch or interrupt reproduction of the butterflies unless at extreme densities, but lives off of the butterfly and replicates itself in order to infect further caterpillars, butterflies and continue the cycle.

It does, however, have consequences. Studies by Sonia Altizer and Karen Oberhauser at the University of Minnesota have shown that butterflies infected with *O. elektroscirrha* have shorter wingspans and weigh less than uninfected butteflies, and heavily infected males had shorter life spans and reduced reproductive success. Intriguingly, they also found a correlation between the prevalence of *O. elektroscirrha* and migratory behavior: populations with higher infection rates had smaller Monarchs who were unable to fly as far as those populations with lower infection rates.

Finally, pathogens such as fungi, viruses and disease organisms also take their toll on butterfly survival. For example, nuclear polyhedris viruses (NPVs) are devastating pathogens that grow in the gut system of caterpillars and eventually kill almost 100 percent of infected individuals. Outwardly there may be no indication that a caterpillar is infected until they stop moving and seemingly dissolve from the inside out. Similarly, fungal spores, naturally occurring bacteria such as *Bacillus thuringiensis* (*Bt—See Pollen, Corn and Monarchs, on page 68*), and other disease organisms, kill large numbers of immature insects. Unfortunately, as with predators, we usually know too little about specific pathogenic threats to Monarchs.

Herbicides and Pesticides

Pesticide and herbicide use is still one of the most important threats to breeding and migrating Monarchs. The statistics—billions and billions of kilograms and liters of this pesticide or that herbicide—are scary, to say the least. Even modern shifts to organic methods of growing and pest control and the use of more targeted biocides (often biological control methods using principles and toxins from naturally occurring sources, such as *Bt*) have not stemmed the tide of pesticide use.

Unfortunately, the majority of crop plants that we grow are veritable monocultures—row upon row of genetically identical plants selected to maximize yield. The problem is that without genetic variation there is no way for identical plants to fight pathogens without the generous use of pesticides, or the incorporation of toxins within the crops themselves. Today we have chemical companies that own patents on specific hybrid strains of common crops setting

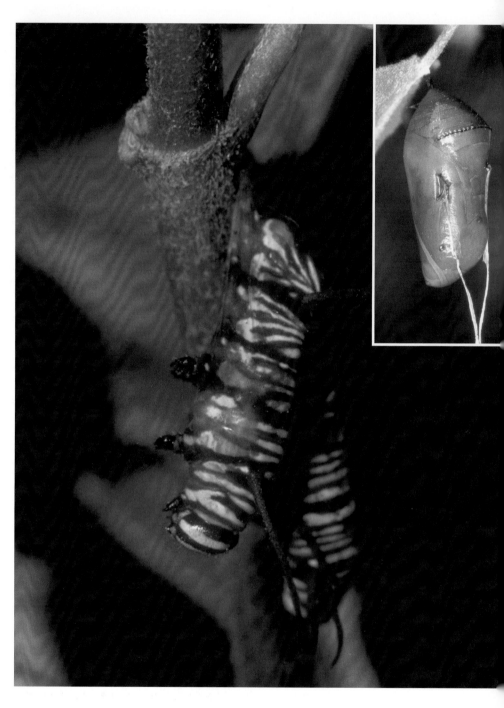

Predators of the Monarch are legion in North America, and can assume many different forms. A Queen larva succumbs to a disease pathogen (above), a Monarch pupa is parasitized by Tachinid flies (inset), and a spider cuts a Monarch loose from its web (opposite). Curiously, the spider will not eat the Monarch after it learns that the butterfly is poisonous.

POLLEN, CORN AND MONARCHS

In 1999, a trio of researchers at Cornell University published a research paper in the journal *Nature* revealing that some hybrid corn plants, genetically modified to include genes from the pathogenic *Bacillus thuringiensis* (*Bt*) as an anti-herbivore defense against foliage-feeding corn earworms and other herbivores of corn, were capable of releasing pollen that included the *Bt* toxin. Because corn is a wind-pollinated species, pollen carrying the toxins was reported to have drifted and deposited on non-target plants at some distance from the source. These non-target plants included the milkweed host plants of Monarchs, and the researchers reported that caterpillars which ate leaves dusted with pollen were more likely to die than those that fed on leaves with corn pollen from unmodified plants or leaves without pollen.

The *Nature* report was abstracted and reported far and wide, creating a controversy in the popular press with the Monarch and genetically modified organisms (GMOs) at its core. It was quickly interpreted (or misinterpreted, as we will see) as direct evidence that humans should "stop playing God" with the genetics of living organisms. Ethical and philosophical considerations aside, how much of an impact could what rapidly became known as "*Bt* corn" have on the Monarch?

A number of studies to confirm and verify the results of the Cornell study—which some complained had serious interpretation and methodological problems—were undertaken. A second report on the effects of *Bt* corn pollen on the Monarch (actually conducted a year before the Cornell paper but published afterward) included an assessment of natural "pollen loads" on potted plants placed near corn fields and used laboratory assays of Monarch caterpillars on leaves dusted with pollen to determine mortality. They conclud-

schedules for the application of specific pesticides—pesticides that they themselves manufacture—at specific times in order to maximize or even obtain a yield. And it's not only big business farms and chemical company profits—individually we may think that we contribute very little to the problem but combined we probably use just as much pesticide on our backyard gardens. Suffice it to say, that pesticide use is rampant throughout the breeding range and migratory routes of the Monarch.

Monarch mortality is also being seen as an indirect consequence—collateral damage, if you will—of pesticide use against other targets, such as control of the imported gypsy moth. These effects are liable to increase with the advent of West Nile virus, a mosquito-borne human pathogen that has recently been

ed that there was significant mortality of Monarch caterpillars. Others in the scientific community were quick to point out, however, that the particular hybrid strains used included one with pollen toxin levels known to be more than 50 times higher than those in other studies.

Subsequent reports, controlling for all of the potential error sources that earlier papers were criticized for, eventually determined that the impact of pollen from the most commonly planted strains of *Bt* corn was essentially nonexistent. Pollen did not travel nearly as far, nor accumulate to high levels, on milkweeds as was supposed. Further, the amount of *Bt* toxin in the pollen was much lower and had little impact when ingested by Monarch caterpillars feeding in areas adjacent to the corn fields. Still, there are some who do not accept the subsequent reports and have elevated the Monarch to the status of an icon for the anti-GMO lobby.

There is little doubt, at the end of this tempest in a teapot, that what was once a little-used, naturally-occurring "biological control pesticide" is now a major pesticide due to its incorporation into so many crop plants. Further effects, although not anticipated, cannot be completely ruled out.

This is not to say that the "*Bt* corn scare" didn't have some effects on the Monarch. Surprisingly, these effects are positive, because as a consequence of the scare a number of intensive studies were conducted to determine how many milkweeds and Monarchs were found in or near cornfields. The result has been a worthwhile increase in our knowledge of the size and extent of the Monarch and milkweed populations through a large proportion of the Monarch breeding range. There is a silver lining to every cloud.

introduced to North America and is now here, I'm afraid, to stay. A recent example of the collateral effect of mosquito spraying was the spraying of permethrin in Gaylord, Minnesota. This small town of 2,000 had permethrin sprayed late in the day, unfortunately at levels higher than those recommended by the manufacturer, and that evening and the following day dying Monarchs were seen by the residents. Subsequent analysis of the dead butterflies confirmed that they contained lethal doses of the pesticide.

The direct action of pesticides on Monarchs is pretty easy to understand: contact in sufficient quantities kills the growing caterpillar, pupa or butterfly; however, there are probably also sub-lethal effects (for example, on lifespan or reproduction) that indirectly impact Monarch populations or migration.

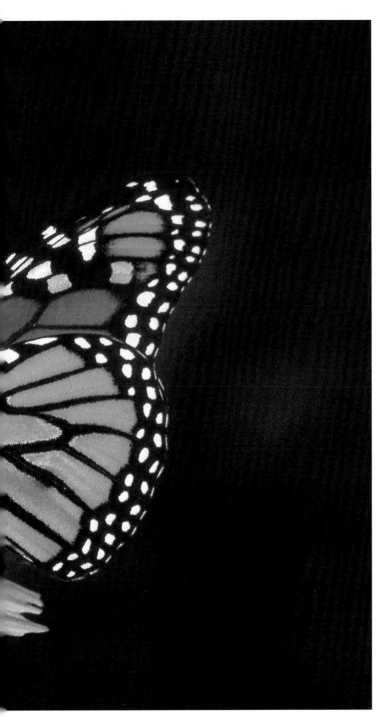

Pesticides and herbicides are two of the most formidable threats to the Monarch in North America. Whether natural or chemical, pesticides directed at other targets, such as gypsy moths or mosquitos, can be deadly to Monarchs, while indiscriminate herbicide use deprives the butterflies of milkweed and flowers for nectaring.

Herbicides, though, work almost entirely indirectly. Milkweed plants sprayed with herbicides may die, and any caterpillars present may starve, but the real effect of herbicides is habitat loss through degradation. Kilometers and kilometers of roadsides are sprayed with herbicides every year as an economical alternative to mowing regimes. Regardless of source or reason, habitat loss remains the main threat facing Monarchs.

Finally, while we have considered the effects of global warming as an environmental concern, the ultimate cause of warming trends is pollution of the environment by gases released as the products of combustion, specifically carbon monoxide, carbon dioxide and ozone. The cumulative but indirect effect of these compounds is to increase the heat retention of the atmosphere, but could there also be direct effects on Monarchs? There are negative effects of ozone on milkweeds and because milkweeds grow along roadsides and the automobile is the most common and prolific polluter that we know, there are likely other effects. The short answer—but the only one we have—is that we just don't know.

Genes and Generations

The issues, threats and problems that face Monarchs and their obligate larval host plants should not be viewed in isolation. Remember that we're talking about four or five *generations* of butterflies here. The generation that survived the winter in Mexico had encountered all of these potential sources of mortality on their journey south and will encounter some of them again as they begin to recolonize the continent. The first spring generation will contend with these issues through their immature stages in northern Mexico and Texas before they too continue the journey north, followed by the second spring generation that must pass through increasingly populated regions and the attendant problems of human competition for land and dominance on its way to the limit of its range expansion.

Similarly, the one or two resident summer generations (depending on whether they are at the southern or northern portions of the breeding range) will have to contend with these issues. These generations are the very antithesis of migratory, since mark-release-recapture studies have shown that these Monarchs stay in one place. Yet despite not traveling over large distances, they are not one whit less endangered. Finally, the migratory generation reappears, again dealing with the trials and tribulations of surviving the immature stages, but also having to survive the exceedingly long migratory flight to return once again—for the first time in their case—to roost in the mountains of the *Sierra Volcanica Transversal* in central Mexico.

What is most fascinating about the multi-generational nature of the eastern North American Monarch's migration is the genetic structure of the populations. Consider for a moment how much or little you resemble your parents and, if you have children, how much or little they resemble you. Every generation is different because parental genotypes mix to form the progeny genotype and not all of any one parent's genes are expressed in their offspring. Now consider that there are four or five *generations* of Monarch butterflies between migrant generations.

There are two intriguing forces at work here. The first and most obvious is that *all* of the butterflies in the migratory generation—the entire population— mates virtually at the same place and time. A thorough mixing of all available genes is completely assured under these conditions, because the chances of any individual butterfly mating with a relative are greatly reduced. On top of this, females frequently continue mating as they travel northward, often mating four or more times, and the multiple paternity of their offspring further dilute and mix the genes.

At the other end of the range, however, there is evidence of genetic differentiation through inbreeding, that is mating between relatives that reinforces some traits in some sub-populations that are different from those in other sub-populations. Yet even five generations is too short a time to generate major changes, and even if there were any minor genetic variations, they would be erased every five generations during the mixing of individuals from all over the breeding range in the fall migration and subsequent random mating during the breakup of the overwintering roosts.

The end result of all this is what has been called a "general-purpose genotype." All of the individuals in the entire population carry a microcosm of all of the genes in the entire population. This kind of variation is generally associated with species that are successful in a wide variety of conditions, including unpredictable changes in environment. It is, I think, one of the potential saving graces of Monarch conservation since it suggests that any genetic bottlenecks—the reduction of the population to a relatively few breeding individuals and the loss of genetic variation not present in those individuals—are less likely to be of major consequence.

Every year scientists tag Monarchs in an effort to monitor changes in the population and migration patterns. Assisting in a tagging project is one way you can help Monarch conservation efforts.

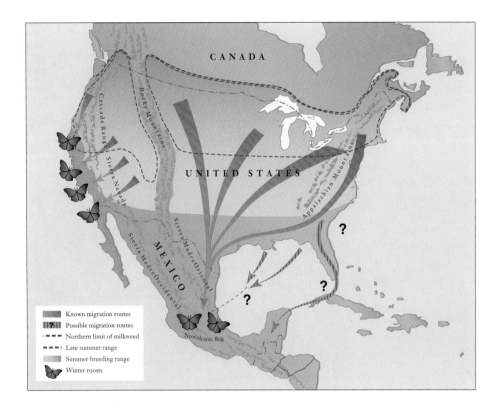

The migration of the Monarch butterfly, Danaus plexippus *(Nymphalidae). Individuals from their late-summer range in Canada must travel up to 2,500 miles (4,000 km) to reach the overwintering grounds in central Mexico.*

Preparations for the long migration southward include converting flower nectar into lipids that can be stored for long periods to sustain life during the journey and long winter ahead. Backyard butterfly gardens often provide needed resourced before they depart and all along the migration routes.

CHAPTER 5

South by Southwest

PAT AND I HAD BEEN VISITING POINT PELEE *National Park, a veritable Mecca for birdwatchers in southwestern Ontario, for only a few years when we went there to do some fall birding in September of 1985. By then, we had quickly lost the "thrill" of just assembling a list of species that we had seen—to our way of thinking this was the next best thing to a useless pursuit—and had quickly become amateur behaviorists. We enjoyed trying to figure out what the creatures that we saw were doing far more than simply identifying them, so it became something of a conundrum for us to consider what we saw the Monarch butterflies doing that day.*

After scanning out off the eastern tip for pelagics we began looking for peeps along the shore (for non-birders, pelagics are ducks and other waterfowl that rarely come close to shore and peeps are, strictly speaking, sandpipers but is also the slang used for just about any shorebird). That's when I first noticed a Monarch gliding along the beach just above the packed sand. As we scanned the beach we then noticed quite a number of Monarchs standing in the sand, one every five or ten meters or so. Every once in a while one would spread its wings and fly a bit, more often than not along the beach, but also out a bit over the water, then return to the beach and set down. Others disappeared around the tip and out of sight.

Now here was a mystery! What were they doing there in the sand? Of course, we were peripherally aware of the migration of the Monarch (but hadn't really thought much about it), but I did know something about other butterfly behaviors so thought that maybe they were puddling for mineral salts. Like all animals, butterflies need salt and because plants contain so little of it, herbivores particularly must seek out salt "licks"— and damp, sandy areas along streams, puddles and other bodies of water are favorite "puddling" areas. We quickly determined that the standing butterflies were not probing the sand with their proboscises but did notice, surprisingly I thought, that they were all facing into the onshore southerly breeze. I had no idea why this might be so we instead asked ourselves where some of them were flying to as they disappeared from view around the tip.

As we followed a few of them around to the west side of the tip we discovered quite a number of sweet clovers, some asters and other wildflowers along with a bevy of nectaring Monarchs. But there were also a fair number of butterflies standing in the sand on this side of the tip, too. A half hour later or so we had determined that there were at least six or seven dozen Monarchs standing or flying along the beach or nectaring on the wildflowers on the two sides of the tip. It was an interesting phenomenon but, at the time, not something that we could fathom.

Later that afternoon, after crossing back to the paved road, we once again made our way back to the tip before heading back to the visitor center. We immediately noticed that there seemed to be fewer butterflies standing on the beach but those that were still there were still facing south, not puddling, and those few that flew out over the water quickly flew back and then around the west side of the tip again. We followed but most of the nectar sources that had attracted the Monarchs earlier in the day were empty of butterflies. Another mystery! Where were the Monarchs going? Then we noticed someone on one of the cross paths gazing through their binoculars up into one of the trees. We went over to see what he was looking at.

To our surprise and delight he wasn't looking at birds at all but a collection of a couple of dozen Monarch butterflies coming to roost for the night. What a strange sight it was to see the tip of a tree branch covered in big orange butterflies. That's when we found out what was going on as he regaled us with the tale of how Monarchs often roost in the trees near the tip of Point Pelee and other peninsulas for a few days while they wait for favorable winds to make the dangerous trip across the open water to continue on their southward journey. Of course, the solution to the mystery and our observations and thoughts about what we had seen that day only raised more questions, but it was those questions and that experience that have led directly to the book you hold in your hand.

The Return Journey

Monarchs in the northern part of the breeding range begin to migrate south as early as late August but reach their peak numbers in mid- to late September, continuing through early October. Their flight style changes remarkably and

Does the Monarch have a "general-purpose genotype?" The alternation of inbreeding in the north—where there is a small, local gene pool—with random mating in the south when the entire population is present gives Monarchs the intriguing ability to adapt to widely varying conditions. Perhaps they will be more resilient to global change and human intrusion than we think.

their movements begin to have a distinct southwestern orientation. Throughout the summer breeding season, Monarchs keep relatively close to the ground while they seek flowers or host plants, and seem to spend about as much time in powered, flapping flight as they do gliding. Yet at the start of migration they begin to spend far more time gliding and fly higher and further between landings. What triggers this change?

As near as can be determined, the onset of migration is "wired" during the caterpillar stage. A combination of the duration and quality of light, falling temperatures and even the quality of their milkweed host plants changes the Monarchs' growth and development so that more energy is channeled to flight muscles and lipid mass and less to the maturation of their sex organs. They emerge from the pupa in a state of reproductive stasis, or diapause, that is, without fully matured sex organs or the procreative drive that accompanies them. In other words, they simply have no interest in mating.

At the same time, the nutrients and energy that would normally have been earmarked for reproduction are shunted to heavier flight muscles and the development of a unique migrational asset: energy storage in the form of fats in a "lipid body" together with the metabolic means of using this stored resource. The lipid mass, held in the abdomen, is balanced by the increased muscle mass of the thorax to maintain their flight "trim" or balance. So the Monarchs emerge as prepared as it's possible to be for their long flight.

It's important to bear in mind that this change is also generational. The three or four preceding generations had typical adult life spans of up to four or five weeks but the migratory generation is different. A side effect of reproductive diapause and the establishment of the metabolic chemistry attending lipid storage is that the normal lifespan is greatly increased, on the order of five to seven times longer than the previous generation's lifespan. So not only are the Monarchs prepared for the long migratory flight but they are also set for an extended stay once they arrive at the overwintering roost.

David Gibo from the University of Toronto at Erindale has been studying flight behavior and the migration of Monarchs in innovative ways, including following them in gliders and ultralight aircraft, using radar, and taking vanishing bearings and body orientation to determine how they maintain their flight direction and compensate for winds. Like hawks, vultures and human gliders, Monarchs spend much of their migration gliding from thermal to thermal, and are known to achieve some pretty respectable altitudes (up to 1,200 m [4,000 ft] above the ground). Also one of the first to study the use and consequences of their lipid mass during migratory flight, Dr. Gibo was astounded to learn that individual butterflies actually compensate for loss of their lipid mass by drinking and storing water. His experience with gliding flight and this research have led him to suggest that Monarchs are not only consummate gliders but are uniquely adapted to migration.

Monarchs appear to use an internal time-compensated compass to determine their current position and ultimate flight direction. What this means is that they basically always seem to know when and where they are and where they're going—even on cloudy days, thanks to the ultraviolet sensitivity of butterfly eyes. Of course, we still have no idea of how or why they migrate to a specific spot over such a long distance, especially given that they are multiple generations away from the last of their species to make the journey. Think about this for a moment—could you find the emigration point of your great-great-grandparents without being able to ask your parents, grandparents and their parents' parents for the necessary directions? A strange and wondrous phenomenon indeed.

Rest Stops

During the extended time period of Monarch migration they must stop and rest, feed or drink daily. Keep in mind that the migrants are being "chased" by winter and the slow but steady decline in the availability of their nectar resources but that they are also no longer constrained by reproductive prerogatives that would consume more of their time than they could otherwise devote to the flight.

Monarchs migrate as individual butterflies, not in small to large flocks, as many birds travel. They also fly much slower—only about 18 km/h (12 mph)—than birds so their migration proceeds at a much less frenetic pace. Of course, birds, as the "hares" in this "tortoise and the hare" race, probably fly quickly between points that are relatively far apart but then spend more time feeding and resting at favorable points along the way. The slower Monarchs also rest and feed along the way, and do not, as a general rule, fly at night as many birds do, but the distances between their rest stops is usually shorter. As a result, like the race between the tortoise and the hare, Monarchs probably arrive at their destinations just as quickly.

Drinking is critical on the southward migration. In addition to finding overnight roost sites, butterflies must seek out water wherever they can. Here a Queen drinks from a drop of overnight dew trapped in the leaves of a seedling partridge pea, Cassia fasciculata (Leguminosae), *in Texas.*

Even though Monarchs migrate as individuals, they're all going in the same direction at the same time so it's inevitable that aggregations form—eventually there *are* "flocks" of migrant Monarchs. As they get closer to their destination and are funneled through a finite area, the size

and number of these aggregations grow and expand. What began as individual butterflies resting overnight or through a storm or other adverse conditions becomes a roost. How these overnight or storm roosts form is something of a mystery. Is there some sort of attraction between individuals, perhaps color, perhaps a scent or pheromone, perhaps some "need" to aggregate that presages the overwhelming numbers that will gather together in the mountains of Mexico? Or is it simply a consequence of many individuals all making the same choices about the best place to rest?

Regardless of how they form, overnight roosts are a characteristic of the southward migration. Roosts generally form on trees that are near to some natural barrier such as a body of water, a canyon or valley, or a southerly point of land. Fred Urquhart, the "grandfather" of Monarch migration studies, suggested that there are three principal factors necessary for a roost: elevation, the size of the trees and the wind direction. How Monarchs know that a body of water is too large to cross against the wind before nightfall is a mystery, however, elevation and tree size seem to make some sense if you consider that the tallest trees, those facing south on the edges of a canyon or water barrier (where they're less likely to be shaded), are where morning sunshine might be the most predictable.

Urquhart presented some evidence suggesting that roosts were most likely to form on the leeward side of a tree where they are protected from drying or chilling winds (although I think that this would also allow them to determine if the wind direction had changed during the night) but this dependence on wind direction somewhat obviates the morning sunshine argument since the leeward side might not be the side that receives the strongest morning sun. Whether there might be some trade-off among the three roost criteria is an interesting— but still unanswered—question.

There have been suggestions and there is much anecdotal evidence that butterflies roost in the same trees over successive years. Urquhart himself tested a variety of ideas—odors left on the trees from previous use, visual attractiveness of Monarchs that had already arrived at the tree, or pheromones used to advertise the locations of roosts—but concluded that the butterflies visually assessed the location and size of the tree, or group of trees, then choose a tree and eventually settle on its leeward side. In his opinion it was not the tree that was attractive but the location, and in instances where individual trees known to have been roost sites in previous years were removed, the migrants simply chose another tree or group of trees nearby.

(OPPOSITE) Roost formation at the overwintering sites begins in early November when Monarchs gather in loose clusters near the tops of the ridges where the Oyamel firs are found. Later in the season the clusters are far denser and are found further down the mountains within the fir forest.

During the extended time period of southward migration Monarchs must stop, rest, feed and drink daily. Here a migrant fall Monarch nectars at floss flower (Eupatorium greggii, Compositae) along the Gulf Coast of Louisiana to replenish needed energy resources.

The number of migrants in individual overnight roosts appears to be strongly correlated with temperature and the passage of cold fronts. Temperatures below 13°C (55°F) with strong, cold winds or low atmospheric pressure seem to produce the largest roosts. Whether larger or more numerous roosts provide some sort of temperature buffering is little known, however, butterfly density—that is how closely packed individual butterflies are within the roost—is also related to temperature. Roost duration is also determined by temperature since at temperatures below 10°C (50°F) the butterflies enter a "state of

10°C (50°F) the butterflies enter a "state of semiparalysis." Thus, morning sunshine *is* an important consideration in roost formation and dissolution.

Full Circle

As the migrants approach the southern United States and northern Mexico, when much of the journey is behind them, the level of their lipid reserves becomes a critical consideration to their ability to survive over the winter. Once again the gauntlet of Texas—that area between the Gulf of Mexico and the western mountains—assumes considerable importance. A certain amount of overlap between breeding range success and the availability of wildflowers in Texas is important. If it has been a good reproductive year and an "easy" migration then a large number of migrants need a large number of wildflowers to refuel on, however, if conditions in Texas have been unfavorable, generally too hot or too dry, then those resources may not be sufficient and more of the migrants will succumb to starvation over the winter.

Dia de los Muertos, the Mexican holiday known as the "Day of the Dead" on November 1 and 2, corresponds quite well with the arrival of the bulk of the migrants to the main roost sites in Michoacan. This is not inconsequential since the locals consider *la mariposa Monarca* to be the souls or spirits of departed relatives that have returned for an annual visit. Robert Pyle has noted that *las palomas*, another name used for the migrant butterflies by people from near the overwintering sites, translates as "the doves, or the souls of the lost children." This interesting juxtaposition of belief, holiday and arrival nicely illustrates that, while the bulk of the world didn't know until 1976 where the eastern North American Monarchs disappeared to in the winter, the native Mexicans did.

Stragglers continue to arrive after the start of November to cluster in loose groups along the ridge tops but by the end of the month the roosts are pretty much set. Given a mid-August departure from their northernmost breeding grounds, and a early to mid-November arrival in Mexico (for those that have survived the trip), we can see that our approximately 90 day estimate for the maximum duration of migration (*See "As the Monarch Flies?" on page 86*) was pretty accurate. Of course, surviving the journey south is only half of the story—they still need to survive through the winter, mate, and then begin a successful return north to bring the migration phenomenon full circle.

AS THE MONARCH FLIES?

The straight line distance that Monarchs travel during migration can be as much as 3,500 km (2,200 mi) as the crow flies. Of course, not all Monarchs have to fly this far—butterflies that begin migration from the southern side of the breeding range have less distance to cover. However, given the need to conserve energy by gliding, the butterflies seek out thermals, circling up in these columns of rising air to a height that lets them glide to the next thermal flowing in the desired direction. They also must spend time (and distance) finding overnight roost sites, taking on water to balance lipid loss (or seeking flowers in order to avoid using stored fats), and avoiding predators. Given all of these factors, and the generally slow flight speed of Monarchs, I wouldn't be at all surprised that some individuals travel twice this distance or more to get to the winter roost sites.

So how long might it take to arrive at the roost sites? Let's try another exercise. During the fall migration, Monarchs appear to average about 75 km (46 mi) per day *in directional flight towards their Mexican destination,* although some tagged butterflies are known to have covered around 130 km (80 mi) in a single day. A simple calculation then, dividing the 3,500 km distance by 75 km per day, suggests that it only takes about 47 days to arrive at the overwintering roosts. However, it is extremely unlikely that any Monarch flies this straight line distance. If my estimate of 7,000 km (4,350 mi) is closer to the actual flight distance traveled then it might take twice as long.

Let's try a different angle: how good is this "guesstimate" of the real flight distance? If we divide the average daily distance by flight speed, about 18 km (12 mi) per hour, it suggests that only one-half of each day, or about 4 hours, of flight is needed to cover the distance. Even if we assume—erring on the side of caution—that individual butterflies actually fly for twice that time during migration—that is they spend 8 hours per day in flight—then they could fly as much as 150 km (about 95 mi) to cover the 75 km average daily distance. This would suggest that individual butterflies might actually fly at least twice the straight line distance, at least 7,000 km (4,350 mi), and the journey will actually take more than 90 days.

The Big Picture

My final point, if you have read this far and aren't yet one of the converted, is to consider the big picture of Monarch conservation and not just the hysteria surrounding one aspect of it. Make no mistake, I believe that strong conservation efforts at the overwintering roost sites in both Mexico and California will go a long way to helping to protect the extraordinary migration of the Monarch butterfly in North America. But given the amount of traffic that Monarchs must cross paths with on their journey, or the loss of suitable overnight roost sites from year to year as we build strip malls, homes and factories, or even the fall cutting of roadside wildflowers in the interests of some misguided sense of "beauty," and it's easy to see that ignoring the migratory flyways and the breeding grounds is a recipe for disaster. A basket that is empty of eggs will remain empty if we don't protect the source of the eggs.

What can you do to help? Don't sit back in your easy chair and depend on others to protect the Monarchs in your backyard. Get involved with local butterfly clubs, assist in tagging, counting and monitoring projects, consult and assist with the growing number of citizen science projects on the Internet (visit **www.monarchwatch.org**, **www.monarchlab.org** or **www.learner.org/jnorth** for ideas, links and information), or lobby and encourage your local, regional, state and national legislators and officials to "do the right thing" wherever and whenever humanly possible. It seems somehow fitting to extend the same level of protection offered to migratory birds and waterfowl to the Monarch butterfly.

Consider working to protect known roost sites, possibly setting up Monarch butterfly reserves to protect significant staging areas, or working to improve the quality and quantity of breeding habitats. On a smaller scale, consider adding some milkweed species and favorite Monarch nectar wildflowers to your garden and using organic methods of pest and weed control. If you get a chance, make the excursion to the Mexican roost sites—I guarantee that it will be one of the most profound experiences in your life. If, standing in that living cathedral, you can turn your back on the Monarch then I will be very surprised (and disappointed).

The tri-national migration of the Monarch underscores the connection that our three peoples have: we share one of the natural wonders of the world. As I wrote in my 1996 Canadian status report, *Distribution, Status and Conservation of the Monarch Butterfly In Canada*, "unilateral conservation efforts will be ineffective in conserving this endangered phenomenon—a concerted international effort is required." Only with dichotomous conservation, that is efforts to allay the many threats and sources of endangerment at *both* the overwintering roosts *and* the breeding grounds, can we be successful at saving the king of North America, this Monarch of the New World.

Monarchs gather at a water source after arriving at their overwintering sites at about the same time as the Mexican Dia de los Muertos, *or Day of the Dead. The locals call the returning migrants* las palomas, *which translates as "the doves" or the "souls of the lost children."*

Glossary

Abdomen The third, most posterior, major body division of insects.

Antenna A segmented sensory organ, found in pairs, above the mouth-parts on the head of an insect. (*plural* Antennae)

Aphrodisiac A male-emitted pheromone that causes a female to prepare for copulation.

Aposematism Warning coloration that is supported by unpalatability or some defense, e.g. chemistry.

Automimicry Mimicry of one's own species in species that vary in palatability due to the presence/absence or strength of some defense.

Basking A method of modifying body temperature or thermoregulating depending on the sun.

Batesian mimicry
Mimicry of an unpalatable model by a palatable mimic.

Biogeography Study of the distribution of organisms.

Camouflage To imitate, or appear to be, the background.

Caredenolides Noxious chemicals present in milkweed host plants (genus *Asclepias*) that protect butterflies from predators.

Caterpillar The second life-history stage of Lepidoptera. Stage at which growth occurs. *See also* larva.

Chrysalis The third life-history stage of Lepidoptera. Stage during which the bulk of metamorphosis occurs. Interchangeable with chrysalid. *See also* pupa.

Cocoon Silken casing around a chrysalis or pupa.

Colony A geographically discrete population or subpopulation of butterflies with determinable boundaries that is separated from other populations.

Common A term used to describe an organism that is abundant, widely distributed, and often encountered.

Community	The assemblage of organisms that interact with each other in some defined habitat.
Cremaster	Hooked structure at the posterior end of a chrysalis used to attach it to a silken pad.
Crochets	Hooks on the prolegs of caterpillars.
Diapause	A period of inactivity and arrested development.
Dispersal	Movements by individuals as part of their daily activities the sum of which are random or non-directional.
Diversity	An ecological term with several meanings. Usually refers to the number of species present in some defined habitat but also refers to the equitability or similarity in abundance of the species.
Dormancy	A period of inactivity.
Eclosion	The emergence of the imago or adult butterfly from the chrysalis or pupa. Sometimes also used to refer to the hatching of a caterpillar or larva from the egg.
Ecology	The study of the factors that determine the distribution and abundance of organisms.
Ecosystem	A biological community in relation to its physical environment.
Egg	The first life-history stage of Lepidoptera and other insects in which a zygote develops into a caterpillar or larva.
Emigrate	To permanently leave a region or area.
Endemic	Limited to a specific area, occurring nowhere else.
Exoskeleton	An outer skeleton as opposed to an endoskeleton or internal skeleton.
Extant	Now living.
Extinct	Having no surviving individuals or populations anywhere.
Extirpated	Having no surviving individuals or populations in an area where they formerly occurred.
Forewing	The anterior pair of wings.
Generation	A discrete but complete life history, e.g. adult to adult via eggs, caterpillars and pupae.
Genitalia	Copulatory organs.
Genus	A taxonomic category in which all species share some defined trait that is not shared by other genera.
Geotactic	Relating to reflexive movement towards the ground.

Habitat	The place where an organism normally lives.
Hairpencil	A specialized organ of butterflies used to disseminate pheromones.
Head	The first, most anterior, major body division of insects.
Herbivore	An animal that feeds exclusively on plants.
Hibernate	A dormancy period through a wet or winter season. Also called overwintering in temperate regions.
Hindwing	The rear pair of wings.
Host plant	The particular food plant of a caterpillar.
Hybrid	The result of a cross between dissimilar parents.
Imago	The fourth and final life-history stage of Lepidoptera. Stage at which reproduction occurs. Also called the adult or butterfly. (*plural* Imagines)
Immature	All life history stages before the reproductive imago or adult stage.
Immigrate	To permanently move to a new region.
Inbreeding	Mating of close relatives, leads to increase in genetic defects.
Instar	Developmental stage between successive molts in an insect.
Larva	The second life-history stage of Lepidoptera. Stage at which growth occurs. *See also* caterpillar.
Lepidoptera	The insect family containing the moths, skippers and butterflies.
Mandibles	Paired chewing mouthparts of a caterpillar.
Metamorphosis	Change in form during development as in the change between a caterpillar and a butterfly.
Metathorax	The third, most posterior, thoracic segment from which the hindwings arise.
Migrant	A participant in a migration.
Migrate	A change in location via directed dispersal by all, or a large proportion, of a population.
Mimetic	An individual that mimics another individual.
Mimicry	A resemblance between individuals that provides some benefit to one or both, e.g. a resemblance between palatable and unpalatable butterflies that protects the palatable individuals from predators.
Molt	The shedding of the exoskeleton that let caterpillars grow.

Monotypic   Having a single form, e.g. a single species in a taxon.

Morph   A single appearance or combination of body form, shape or color.

Müllerian mimicry

A mimetic system wherein all participants are unpalatable and share a single morph.

Muscular thermogenesis

Shivering to generate heat in the muscles.

Mutation   Heritable changes that differ from that most commonly encountered.

Nearctic   Temperate and arctic North America.

Neotropic   Tropical North, Central and South America.

Overwinter   To hibernate.

Oviposition   The process by which a female butterfly chooses a site to lay eggs. Also used to describe the act of egg laying.

Ovum   A single egg. (*plural* Ova)

Parasite   An organism that lives off of another organism but does not kill it.

Parasitioid   An organism that kills another organism by living off of it.

Perch   A passive mate location strategy characterized by waiting at landmark sites for the passing of potential mates.

Pheromones   Specialized chemical compounds that promote behavioral responses by other individuals.

Photoperiod   The length of the day/night cycle.

Phototactic   Relating to reflexive movement towards the light.

Population   An interbreeding group of individuals of the same species that are separated in space or time from other groups of the same species.

Predator   An organism that eats another organism.

Prepupa   A resting stage within the last larval instar prior to pupation.

Proboscis   The coiled, straw-like sucking tube mouthparts of a butterfly. Also called the haustellum.

Prolegs   The fleshy abdominal legs of caterpillars.

Pupa   The developmental stage between a larva (caterpillar) and an imago (adult butterfly). *See also* Chrysalis. (*plural* Pupae or pupas)

Refuge An area that has remained unchanged while areas around it have changed markedly, often serving as a refuge for species with specific habitat requirements.

Roost A gathering place of resting butterflies.

Scent scales Specialized, highly modified scales, usually on the wings, that produce chemical compounds that act as sex pheromones, aphrodisiacs or attractants. Also called androconial scales.

Segment Structural units of invertebrate bodies, as in the segments of caterpillars, antennae, etc.

Seta A moveable sensory hair. (*plural* Setae)

Species Any group of interbreeding organisms that are differentiated from other such reproductive groups. Also a taxonomic category in which all organisms of the same species are considered different from all other species.

Stray An individual that is found far outside its usual range but is not a common emigrant.

Subspecies A distinctive subset of a species, may be geographic in origin. Sometimes considered a variety or race.

Super A prefix meaning above or over, as in a superfamily (between family and order).

Taxon An individual unit in a taxonomic classification, e.g. a species, a genus or any other identifiable group. (*plural* Taxa)

Temperate An area with a mean annual temperature of between 10°C and 13°C (50°F and 55°F).

Territory A living space that has evolutionary consequences to individuals, e.g. a territory enhances either the survival or the reproduction of a territorial individual.

Thermoregulation
 The process of regulating body temperature.

Thorax The second, center, major body division of the insect body, contains the bulk of the locomotory muscles, legs and wings.

Tropical An area with a mean annual temperature above 25°C (75°F) where no freezing occurs.

Tropics The latitudinal region between the Tropic of Cancer, 23.5°N latitude, and the Tropic of Capricorn, 23.5°S latitude.

Tubercle A bump or knob on a caterpillar's body.

Type   Taxonomic term for the individual upon which a species description is based.

Ultraviolet   Wavelengths of light that are beyond the human visual spectrum but visible to some insects.

Warning coloration

Colors used to advertise unpalatability, regardless of the palatability of the advertiser. Usually combinations of black with white, red, orange or yellow, often in alternating bands.

Bibliography

For those of you who are interested in delving into the primary research on the Monarch, the following bibliography provides the sources that I consulted for this book. If you are interested in learning more but would prefer less academic emphasis, then I suggest you consult my previous work, *A World for Butterflies*, and the books that follow.

Books

Ackery, P. R. and Vane-Wright, R. I. *Milkweed Butterflies: Their Cladistics and Biology.* Ithaca: British Museum (Natural History)/Cornell University Press, 1984.

Douglas, M. M. *The Lives of Butterflies.* Ann Arbor: University of Michigan Press, 1986.

Halpern, S. *Four Wings and a Prayer: Caught in the Mystery of the Monarch Butterfly.* New York: Pantheon Books, 2001.

Malcolm, S. B. and Zalucki, M. P. (ed.) *Biology and Conservation of the Monarch Butterfly.* Science Series Vol. 38. Los Angeles: Natural History Museum of Los Angeles County, 1993

New, T. R. *Butterfly Conservation.* Melbourne: Oxford University Press, 1991.

Pyle, R. M. *Chasing Monarchs: Migrating With the Butterflies of Passage.* New York: Houghton-Mifflin, 1999.

Rea, B., Oberhauser, K. and Quinn, M. A. *Milkweed, Monarchs and More: a Field Guide to the Invertebrate Community in the Milkweed Patch.* Glenshaw: Bas Relief Publishing Group, 2003

Schappert, P. J. *A World for Butterflies: Their Lives, Behavior and Future.* Toronto: Key Porter Books, 2001.

Urquhart, F. A. *The Monarch Butterfly: International Traveler.* Chicago: Nelson-Hall, Inc., 1987.

Articles and Papers

Ackery, P. R. and Vane-Wright, R. I. "Patterns of plant utilization by danaine butterflies."

in *Proceedings of the Congress of European Lepidopterology 1982* (1985): 3–7.

Alonso-Mejia, A. and Brower, L. P. "From model to mimic: age-dependent unpalatability in Monarch butterflies." *Experientia* 50 (1994): 176–181.

Altizer, S. M. "Migratory behavior and host-parasite co-evolution in natural populations of Monarch butterflies infected with a protozoan parasite." *Evolutionary Ecology Research* 3 (2001): 611–632.

—. and Oberhauser, K. S. "Effects of the protozoan parasite *Ophryocystis elektroscirrha* on the fitness of Monarch butterflies (*Danaus plexippus*)." *Journal of Invertebrate Pathology* 74 (1999): 76–88.

—. ; Oberhauser, K. S. and Brower, L. P. "Associations between host migration and the prevalence of a protozoan parasite in natural populations of adult Monarch butterflies." *Ecological Entomology* 25 (2000): 125–139.

Anderson, J. B. and Brower, L. P. "Freeze-protection of overwintering Monarch butterflies in Mexico: critical role of the forest as a blanket and an umbrella." *Ecological Entomology* 21 (1996): 107–116.

Barker, J. F. and Herman, W. S. "Effect of photoperiod and temperature on reproduction of the Monarch butterfly, *Danaus plexippus*." *Journal of Insect Physiology* 22 (1976): 1565–1568.

Beall, G. "The fat content of a butterfly, *Danaus plexippus* Linn., as affected by migration." *Ecology* 29 (1948): 80–94.

Berenbaum, M. R. "Aposematism and mimicry in caterpillars." *Journal of the Lepidopterists' Society* 49 (1995): 386–396.

—. and Miliczky, E. "Mantids and milkweed bugs: efficacy of aposematic coloration against invertebrate predators." *American Midland Naturalist* 111 (1984): 64–68.

Blakley, N. R. and Dingle, H. "Competition: butterflies eliminate milkweed bugs from a Caribbean Island." *Oecologia* 37 (1978): 133–136.

Boggs, C. L. and Gilbert, L. E. "Male contribution to egg production in butterflies: evidence for transfer of nutrients at mating." *Science* 206 (1989): 83–84.

Bolsinger, M., Lier, M. E. and Hughes, P. R. "Influence of ozone air pollution on plant-herbivore interactions. Part 2: Effects of ozone on feeding preference, growth and consumption rates of Monarch butterflies (*Danaus plexippus*)." *Environmental Pollution* 77 (1992): 31–37.

Boppre, M. "Chemical communication, plant relationships and mimicry in the evolution of Danaid butteflies." *Entomologia Experimentalis et Applicata* 24 (1978): 64–77.

—. "Adult lepidoptera 'feeding' at withered *Heliotropium* plants (Boraginaceae) in East

Africa." *Ecological Entomology* 6 (1981): 449–452.

—. "Leaf-scratching—a specialized behaviour of danaine butterflies (Lepidoptera) for gathering secondary plant substances." *Oecologia* 59 (1983): 414–416.

—. "Lepidoptera and pyrrolizidine alkaloids: Exemplification of complexity in chemical ecology." *Journal of Chemical Ecology* 16 (1990): 165–185.

Borkin, S. S. "Notes on shifting distribution patterns and survival of immature *Danaus plexippus* (Lepidoptera: Danaidae) on the food plant *Asclepias syriaca*." Great Lakes Entomologist 15 (1982): 199–206.

Brower, A. V. Z. and Boyce, T. M. "Mitochondrial DNA variation in Monarch butterflies." *Evolution* 45 (1991): 1281–1286.

Brower, L. P. "Experimental analyses of egg cannibalism in the Monarch and Queen butterflies, *Danaus plexippus* and *D. gilippus berenice*." *Physiological Zoology* 34 (1961): 287–296.

—. "Ecological chemistry." *Scientific American* 220 (1969): 22–29.

—. "Monarch migration." *Natural History* 84 (1977): 40–53.

—. "Chemical defense in butterflies. In *The Biology of Butterflies*, ed. R. I. Vane-Wright and P. R. Ackery., pp. 109–134. London: Academic Press, 1984.

—. "New perspectives on the migration biology of the Monarch butterfly, *Danaus plexippus* L. *Contributions in Marine Science Supplement* 27 (1985): 748–785.

—. "Understanding and misunderstanding the migration of the Monarch butterfly (Nymphalidae) in North America: 1857-1995." *Journal of the Lepidopterists' Society* 49 (1995): 304–385.

—. "Monarch butterfly orientation: missing pieces of a magnificent puzzle." *Journal of Experimental Biology* 199 (1996): 93–103.

—. "Canary in the Cornfield: the Monarch and the *Bt* corn controversy." Orion (2001). www.oriononline.org/pages/om/01-2om/01-2om_canary.html

—. and Calvert, W. H. "Foraging dynamics of bird predators on overwintering Monarch butterflies in Mexico." *Evolution* 39 (1985): 852–868.

—. ; Calvert, W. H., Hedrick, L. E. and Christian, J. "Biological observations on an overwintering colony of Monarch butterflies (*Danaus plexippus*, L., Danaidae) in Mexico. *Journal of the Lepidopterists' Society* 31 (1977): 232–242.

—. ; Fink, L. S., Van Zandt Brower, A., Leong, K., Oberhauser, K., et al. "Roundtable: On the dangers of interpopulational transfers of Monarch butterflies." *Bioscience* 45 (1995): 540–544.

—. and Glazier, S. C. "Localization of heart poisons in the Monarch butterfly." Science 188 (1975): 19–25.

—. ; Horner, B. E., Marty, M. A., Moffitt, C. M. and Bernardo, V. R. "Mice (*Peromyscus maniculatus, P. spicilegus*, and *Microtus mexicanus*) as predators of overwintering Monarch butterflies (*Danaus plexippus*) in Mexico." *Biotropica* 17 (1985): 89–99.

—. and Malcolm, S. B. "Animal migrations: Endangered phenomena." *American Zoologist* 31 (1991): 265–276.

Brown, J. J. and Chippendale, G. M. "Migration of the Monarch butterfly, *Danaus plexippus*:energy sources." *Journal of Insect Physiology* 20 (1974): 1117–1130.

Bull, C. M., Zalucki, M. P., Suzuki, Y., Mackay, D. A. and Kitching, R. L. "An experimental investigation of resource use by female Monarch butterflies, *Danaus plexippus* (L.)." *Australian Journal of Ecology* 10 (1985): 391–398.

Calvert, W. H. "Behavioral response of Monarch butterflies (Nymphalidae) to disturbances in their habitat: a startle response?" *Journal of the Lepidopterists' Society* 48 (1994): 157–165.

—. "Fire ant predation on Monarch larvae (Nymphalidae: Danainae) in a central Texas prairie." *Journal of the Lepidopterists' Society* 50 (1996): 149–151.

—. "Patterns in the spatial and temporal use of Texas milkweeds (Asclepiadaceae) by the Monarch butterfly (*Danaus plexippus* L.) during Fall, 1996." *Journal of the Lepidopterists' Society* 53 (1999): 37–44.

—. and Brower, L. P. "The location of Monarch butterfly (*Danaus plexippus* L.) overwintering colonies in Mexico in relation to topography and climate." *Journal of the Lepidopterists' Society* 40 (1986): 164–187.

—. ; Zuchowski, W. and Brower, L. P. "The impact of forest thinning on microclimate in Monarch butterfly (*Danaus plexippus* L.) overwintering areas of Mexico." *Boletin de la Sociedad Botanica de Mexico* 42 (1982): 11–18.

—. ; Zuchowski, W. and Brower, L. P. "The effect of rain, snow and freezing temperatures on overwintering Monarch butterflies in Mexico." *Biotropica* 15 (1983): 42–47.

Cohen, J. A. "Differences and similarities in cardenolide content of Queen and Monarch butterflies in Florida and their ecological and evolutionary implications." *Journal of Chemical Ecology* 11 (1985): 85–103.

—. and Brower, L. P. "Oviposition and larval success of wild Monarch butterflies (Lepidoptera: Danaidae) in relation to host plant size and cardenolide concentration." *Journal of the Kansas Entomological Society* 55 (1982): 343–348.

Dethier, V. G. "The Monarch revisited." *Journal of the Kansas Entomological Society* 48 (1975): 129–140.

—. "Mechanism of host-plant recognition." *Entomologia Experimentalis et Applicata* 31 (1982): 49–56.

DiTommaso, A. and Losey, J. E. "Oviposition preference and larval performance of Monarch butterflies (*Danaus plexippus*) on two invasive swallow-wort species." *Entomologia Experimentalis et Applicata* 108 (2003): 205–209.

Drummond, B. A. "Multiple mating and sperm competition in the Lepidoptera." In *Sperm Competetion and the Evolution of Animal Mating Systems*, ed. R. L. Smith. pp. 291–370. Orlando: Academic Press, 1984.

Dudley, R. and Adler, G. H. "Biogeography of milkweed butterflies (Nymphalidae, Danainae) and mimetic patterns on tropical Pacific archipelagos." *Journal of the Linnean Society* 57 (1996): 317–326.

Dussourd, D. E. and Denno, R. F. "Deactivation of plant defense: Correspondence between insect behavior and secretory canal architecture." *Ecology* 72 (1991): 1383–1396.

Eanes, W. F. "Morphological variance and enzyme heterozygosity in the Monarch butterfly." *Nature* 276 (1978): 263–264.

—. and Koehn, R. K. "An analysis of genetic structure in the Monarch butterfly, *Danaus plexippus* L." *Evolution* 32 (1978): 784–797.

Edgar, J. A. and Culvenor, C. C. J. "Pyrrolizidine ester alkaloids in Danaid butterflies." *Nature* 248 (1974): 614–616.

Edgar, J. A., Culvenor, C. C. J. and Pliske, T. E. "Co-evolution of Danaid butterflies with their host plants. *Nature* 250 (1974): 646–648.

Eisner, T. and Meinwald, J. "Alkaloid-derived pheromones and sexual selection in Lepidoptera." In *Pheromone Biochemistry*, ed. G. D. Prestwich and G. J. Blomquist. pp. 251–269. Orlando: Academic Press, 1987.

Fink, L. S. and Brower, L. P. "Birds can overcome the cardenolide defence of Monarch butterflies in Mexico." *Nature* 291 (1981): 67–70.

Fink, L. S., Brower, L. P., Waide, R. B., and Spitzer, P. R. "Overwintering Monarch butterflies as food for insectivorous birds in Mexico." *Biotropica* 15 (1981): 151–153.

Funk, R. S. "Overwintering of Monarch butterflies as a breeding colony in southwestern Arizona." *Journal of the Lepidopterists' Society* 22 (1968): 63–64.

Gibo, D. L. "Flight strategies of migrating Monarch butterflies (*Danaus plexippus* L.) in southern Ontario." In *Insect Flight: Dispersal and Migration*, ed. W. Danthanarayana. pp. 172–184. Berlin: Springer-Verlag, 1986.

—. and McCurdy, J. A. "Evidence for use of water ballast by Monarch butterflies, *Danaus plexippus* (Nymphalidae)." *Journal of the Lepidopterists' Society* 47 (1993): 154–160.

—. and McCurdy, J. A. "Lipid accumulation by migrating Monarch butterflies (*Danaus plexippus* L.). *Canadian Journal of Zoology* 71 (1993): 76–82.

—. and Pallett, M. J. "Soaring flight of Monarch butterflies, *Danaus plexippus* (Lepidoptera: Danaidae), during the late summer migration in southern Ontario." *Canadian Journal of Zoology* 57 (1979): 1393–1401.

Glendinning, J. I., Alonso, A. and Brower, L. P. "Behavioral and ecological interaction of foraging mice (*Peromyscus melanotis*) with overwintering Monarch butterflies (*Danaus plexippus*) in Mexico." *Oecologia* 75 (1988): 222–227.

Glendinning, J. I. and Brower, L. P. "Feeding and breeding responses of five mice species to overwintering aggregations of the Monarch butterfly." *Journal of Animal Ecology* 59 (1990): 1091–1112.

Hansen Jesse, L. C. and Obrycki, J. J. "Field deposition of *Bt* transgenic corn pollen: lethal effects on the Monarch butterfly." Oecologia 125 (2000): 241–248.

Haribal, M. and Renwick, J. A. A. "Oviposition stimulants for the Monarch butterfly: Flavonol glycosides from *Asclepias curassavica*." *Phytochemistry* 41 (1996): 139–144.

Hartzler, R. G. and Buhler, D. D. "Occurrence of common milkweed (*Asclepias syriaca*) in cropland and adjacent areas." *Crop Protection* 19 (2000): 363–366.

Hayes, J. L. "A study of the relationships of diapause phenomena and other life history characters in temperate butterflies." *American Naturalist* 120 (1982): 160–170.

Herman, W. S. "Body weight and wing length changes in Minnesota populations of the Monarch butterfly." *Journal of the Lepidopterists' Society* 42 (1988): 32–36.

—. and Barker, J. F. "Effect of mating on Monarch butterfly oogenesis." *Experientia* 33 (1977): 688–689.

—. ; Brower, L. P. and Calvert, W. H. "Reproductive tract development in Monarch butterflies overwintering in California and Mexico." *Journal of the Lepidopterists' Society* 43 (1989): 50–58.

—. ; Lessman, C. A. and Johnson, G. D. "Correlation of juvenile hormone titer changes with reproductive tract development in the posteclosion Monarch butterfly." *Journal of Experimental Zoology.* 218 (1981): 387–395.

—. and Peng, P. "Juvenile hormone stimulation of sperm activator production in male Monarch butterflies." *Journal of Insect Physiology* 22 (1976): 579–581.

Hill, H. F., Wenner, A. M., and Wells, P. H. "Reproductive behavior in an overwintering aggregation of Monarch butterflies." *American Midland Naturalist* 95 (1976): 10–19.

Hobson, K. A., Wassenaar, L. I. and Taylor, O. R. "Stable isotopes (ΔD and ^{13}C) are geographic indicators of natal origins of Monarch butterflies in eastern North America." *Oecologia* 120 (1999): 397–404.

Hughes, J. M. and Zalucki, M. P. "Genetic variation in a continuously breeding population of *Danaus plexippus* L. (Lepidoptera: Nymphalidae)." *Heredity* 52 (1984): 1–7.

—. "The relationship between the Pgi Locus and the ability to fly at low temperatures in the Monarch butterfly *Danaus plexippus*." *Biochemical Genetics* 31 (1993): 521–532.

Jeffords, M. R., Sternburg, J. G. and Waldbauer, G. P. "Batesian mimicry: field demonstration of the survival value of Pipevine Swallowtail and Monarch colour patterns." *Evolution* 33 (1979): 275–286.

Kammer, A. E. "Thoracic temperature, shivering, and flight in the Monarch butterfly, *Danaus plexippus* (L.)." *Z. Vergl. Physiologie* 68 (1970): 334–344.

—. "Influence of acclimation temperature on the shivering behaviour of the butterfly *Danaus plexippus* (L.)." *Z. Vergl. Physiologie* 72 (1971): 364–369.

Kanz, J. E. "The orientation of migrant and non-migrant Monarch butterflies, *Danaus plexippus* (L.)." *Psyche* 84 (1977): 120–141.

Kitching, I. J. "Early stages and the classification of the milkweed butterflies (Lepidoptera: Danainae)." *Zoological Journal of the Linnean Society* 85 (1985): 1–97.

Kitching, R. L. and Zalucki, M. P. "A cautionary note on the use of oviposition records as larval food-plant records." *Australian Entomological Magazine* 10 (1983): 64–66.

Knight, A. "Spring remigration of the Monarch butterfly, *Danaus plexippus* (Lepidoptera: Nymphalidae), in north-central Florida: estimating population parameters using mark-recapture." *Biological Journal of the Linnean Society* 68 (1999): 531–556.

Leong, K. L. H., Yoshimura, M. A. Kaya, H. KI. and Williams, H. 1997. Instar susceptibility of the Monarch butterfly (*Danaus plexippus*) to the Neogregarine parasite, *Ophryocystis elektroscirrha*. Journal of Invertebrate Pathology 69: 79–83.

Loosey, J. E., Raynor, L. S. and Carter, M. E. "Transgenic pollen harms Monarch larvae." Nature 399 (1999): 214.

Madson, C. "Monarch. Before its migration, the Monarch must survive the dangers of simply becoming a butterfly." *Wyoming Wildlife* 55 (1991): 4–9.

Malcolm, S. B. "Monarch butterfly migration in North America: Controversy and conservation." *Trends in Ecology and Evolution 2* (1987): 135–138.

—. "Mimicry: status of a classical evolutionary paradigm." *Trends in Ecology and Evolution 5* (1990): 57–62.

—. "Milkweeds, Monarch butterflies and the ecological significance of cardenolides." *Chemoecology* 5/6 (1994): 101–117.

—. and Brower, L. P. "Selective oviposition by Monarch butterflies (*Danaus plexippus* L.) in a mixed stand of *Asclepias curassavica* L. and *A. incarnata* L. in south Florida." *Journal of the Lepidopterists' Society* 40 (1986): 255–263.

—. and Brower, L. P. "Evolutionary and ecological implications of cardenolide seques-tration in the Monarch butterfly." *Experientia* 45 (1989): 284–295.

—. ; Cockrell, B. J. and Brower, L. P. "Monarch butterfly voltinism: Effects of tempera-ture constraints at different latitudes." *Oikos* 49 (1987): 77–82.

Masters, A. R., Malcolm. S. B. and Brower, L. P. "Monarch butterfly (*Danaus plexippus*) thermoregulatory behavior and adaptations for overwintering in Mexico." *Ecology* 69 (1988): 458–467.

Mathavan, S. and Bhaskaran, R. "Food selection and utilization in a danaid butterfly." *Oecologia* 18 (1975): 55–62.

Mathavan, S., Pandian, T. J. and Mary, M. J. "Use of feeding rate as an indicator of caloric value in some lepidopterous larvae." *Oecologia* 24 (1976): 91–94.

Matthews, D. "Mountain Monarchs: In the Mexican highlands, Monarch butterflies by the millions awaken to the warming spring sun." *Wildlife Conservation* 95 (1992): 26–29.

Mattila, H. R. and Otis, G. W. "A comparison of the host preference of Monarch butter-flies (*Danaus plexippus*) for milkweed (*Asclepias syriaca*) over dog-strangler vine (*Vincetoxicum rossicum*)." *Entomologia Experimentalis et Applicata* 107 (2003): 193–199.

McIsaac, H. P. "The capture and release of a Monarch butterfly (Nymphalidae: Danainae) by a barn swallow." *Journal of the Lepidopterists' Society* 45 (1991): 62–63.

McKenna, D. D., McKenna, K. M., Malcolm, S. B. and Berenbaum, M. R. "Mortality of Lepidoptera along roadways in central Illinois." *Journal of the Lepidopterists' Society* 55 (2001): 63–68.

McLaughlin, R. E. and Myers, J. E. "*Ophryocystis elektroscirrha* sp. n., a neogregarine pathogen of the Monarch butterfly, *Danaus plexippus* (L.), and the Florida Queen butterfly, *D. gilippus berenice* (Cramer)." *Journal of Protozoology* 17 (1970): 300–305.

Myers, J. "Pheromones and courtship behaviour in butterflies." *American Zoologist* 12 (1972): 545–551.

—. and Brower, L. P. "A behavioural analysis of the courtship pheromone receptors of the Queen butterfly, *Danaus gilippus berenice*." *Journal of Insect Physiology* 15 (1969): 2117–2130.

Neck, R. W. "Summer Monarch (*Danaus plexippus*) in southern Texas (Danaidae)." *Journal of the Lepidopterists' Society* 30 (1976): 137.

—. "Lepidoptera foodplant records from Texas." *Journal of Research On the Lepidoptera* 15 (1976): 75–82.

Oberhauser, K. S. "Male Monarch butterfly spermatophore mass and mating strategies."

Animal Behaviour 36 (1988): 1384–1388.

—. "Effects of spermatophores on male and female Monarch butterfly reproductive success." *Behavioral Ecology and Sociobiology* 25 (1989): 237–246.

—. "Rate of ejaculate breakdown and intermating intervals in Monarch butterflies." *Behavioral Ecology and Sociobiology* 31 (1992): 367–373.

—. "Fecundity, lifespan and egg mass in butterflies: effects of male-derived nutrients and female size." *Functional Ecology* 11 (1997): 166–175.

—. and Hampton, R. "The relationship between mating and oogenesis in Monarch butterflies (Lepidoptera: Danainae)." *Journal of Insect Behavior* 8 (1995): 701–713.

—. and Peterson, A. T. "Modeling current and future potential wintering distributions of eastern North American Monarch butterflies." Proceedings of the National Academy of Sciences (Washington), 100 (24) (2003): 14063–14068.

—. ; Prysby, M. D., Mattila, H. R., Stanley-Horn, D. E. Sears, M. K., Dively, G., Olson, E. Pleasants, J. M., Lam, W. F. and Hellmich, R. L. "Temporal and spatial overlap between Monarch larvae and corn pollen." Proceedings of the National Academy of Sciences (Washington), 98 (21) (2001): 11913–11918.

Ogarrio, R. "Development of the civic group, Pro Monaraca, A. C., for the protection of the Monarch butterfly wintering grounds in the Republic of Mexico." *Atala* 9 (1984): 11–13.

Parmesan, C., Ryrholm, N., Stefanescu, C., Hill, J. K., Thomas, C. D., Descimon, H., Huntley, B., Kaila, L., Kullberg, J., Tammaru T., Tennent, W. J., Thomas, J. A. and Warren M. "Poleward shifts in geographical ranges of butterfly species associated with regional warming." *Nature* 399 (6736) (1999): 579–583.

Platt, A. P., Coppinger, R. P. and Brower, L. P. "Demonstration of the mimetic advantage of edible butterflies presented to caged avian predators." *American Zoology* 9 (1969): 1062.

Platt, A. P., Coppinger, R. P. and Brower, L. P. "Demonstration of the selective advantage of mimetic *Limenitis* butterflies presented to caged avian predators." *Evolution* 25 (1971): 692–701.

Pliske, T. E. "Courtship behaviour of the Monarch butterfly, *Danaus plexippus* L." *Annals of the Entomological Society of America* 68 (1975): 143–151.

—. and Eisner, T. "Sex pheromone of the Queen butterfly: biology." *Science* 164 (1969): 1170–1172.

Price, P. W. and Wilson, M. F. "Abundance of herbivores on six milkweed species in Illinois." *American Midland Naturalist* 101 (1979): 76–86.

Pyle, R. M. "International efforts for Monarch conservation, and conclusion." *Atala* 9

(1984): 21–22.

—."Las Monarcas: butterflies on thin ice." Orion (2001). www.oriononline.org/pages/ om/01-2om/01-2om_monarcas.html

Ritland, D. B. "Palatability of aposematic Queen butterflies (*Danaus gilippus*) feeding on *Sarcostemma clausum* (Asclepiadaceae) in Florida." *Journal of Chemical Ecology* 17 (1991): 1593–1610.

—. "Revising a classic butterfly mimicry scenario: Demonstration of Mullerian mimicry between Florida Viceroys (*Limenitis archippus floridensis*) and Queen (*Danaus gilippus berenice*)." *Evolution* 45 (1991): 918–934.

—. "Variation in palatability of Queen butterflies (*Danaus gilippus*) and implications regarding mimicry." *Ecology* 75 (1994): 732–746.

—. and Brower, L. P. "The Viceroy butterfly is not a batesian mimic. *Nature* 350 (1991): 497–498

Roeske, C. M., Seiber, J. N., Brower, L. P. and Moffitt, C. M. "Milkweed cardenolides and their comparative processingby Monarch butterflies (*Danaus plexippus* L.)." *Recent Advances in Phytochemistry* 10 (1976): 93–167.

Ross, G. N. "The Monarch: what's in a name?" *News of the Lepidopterists' Society* 32 (2001): 20–21.

Rothschild, M. "Hell's angels." *Antenna* 2 (1978): 38–39.

—. ; Gardiner, B. and Mummery, R. "Pupal colouration and diet." *Antenna* 2 (1978): 15.

—. and Marsh, N. "Some peculiar aspects of danaid/plant relationships." *Entomologia Experimentalis et Applicata* 24 (1978): 637–650.

Rutowski, R. H., Newton, M. and Schaefer, J. "Interspecific variation in the size of the nutrient investment made by male butterflies during copulation." *Evolution* 37 (1983): 708–713.

Sakai, W. H. "Avian predation on Monarch butterfly, *Danaus plexippus* (Nymphalidae: Danainae), at a California overwintering site." *Journal of the Lepidopterists' Society* 48 (1994): 148–156.

Sauer, P. "The Monarch versus the Global Empire." Orion (2001). www.oriononline.org/ pages/om/01-2om/01-2om_monarch.html

Schappert, P. J. "Distribution, Status and Conservation of the Monarch Butterfly, *Danaus plexippus* (L.), in Canada." (1996): www.esb.utexas.edu/philjs/Monarch/ MONREP97.html

Schroeder, L. A. "Energy, matter and nitrogen utilization by the larvae of the Monarch butterfly *Danaus plexippus.*" *Oikos* 27 (1976): 259–264.

—. "Energy, matter and nitrogen utilization by larvae of the milkweed tiger-moth,

Euchaetias egle." *Oikos* 28 (1977): 27–31.

Shapiro, A. M. "Avian predation on butterflies—again." *Entomologist's Record and Journal of Variation* 89 (1977): 293–295.

Shelton, A. M. and Sears, M. K. "The Monarch butterfly controversy: scientific interpretations of a phenomenon." *The Plant Journal* 27 (2001): 483–488.

Shephard, J. M., Hughes, J. M. and Zalucki, M. P. "Genetic differentiation between Australian and North American populations of the Monarch butterfly, *Danaus plexippus* (L.) (Lepidoptera: Nymphalidae): an exploration using allozyme electrophoresis." *Biological Journal of the Linnean Society* 75 (2002): 437–452.

Shields, O. and Emmel, J. F. "A review of carrying pair behaviour and mating times in butterflies." *Journal of Research On the Lepidoptera* 12 (1973): 25–64.

Solensky, M. J. and Larkin, E. "Temperature-induced variation in larval coloration in *Danaus plexippus* (Lepidoptera: Nymphalidae)." *Annals of the Entomological Society of America* 96 (2003): 211–216.

Stimson, J. and Meyers, L. "Inheritance and frequency of a color polymorphism in *Danaus plexippus* (Lepidoptera: Danaidae) on Ohahu, Hawaii." *Journal of Research on the Lepidoptera* 23 (1984): 153–160.

Stimson, J. and Berman, M. "Predator induced colour polymorphism in *Danaus plexippus* L. (Lepidoptera: Nymphalidae) in Hawaii." *Heredity* 65 (1990): 401–406.

Stimson, J. and Kasuya, M. "Decline in the frequency of the white morph of the Monarch butterfly (Danaus plexippus plexippus L., Nymphalidae) on Oahu, Hawaii." *Journal of the Lepidopterists' Society* 54 (2000): 29–32.

Suzuki, Y. and Zalucki, M. P. "The influence of sex ratio on female dispersal in *Danaus plexippus* (L.) (Lepidoptera: Danaidae)." *Journal of the Australian Entomological Society* 25 (1986): 31–35.

Svard, L. and Wiklund, C. "Fecundity, egg weight and longevity in relation to multiple matings in females of the Monarch butterfly." *Behavioral Ecology and Sociobiology* 23 (1988): 39–43.

—. "Prolonged mating in the Monarch butterfly *Danaus plexippus* and nightfall as a cue for sperm transfer." *Oikos* 52 (1988): 351–354.

—. "Mass and production weight of ejaculates in relation to monandry/polyandry in butterflies." *Behavioral Ecology and Sociobiology* 24 (1989): 395–402.

Swengel, A. B. "Population fluctuations of the Monarch (*Danaus plexippus*) in the 4th of July butterfly count 1977–1994." *American Midland Naturalist* 134 (1995): 205–214.

Tarrier, M. "Protection of lepidopterans: SOS Monarchs: last act: the farewell (Lepidoptera Nymphalidae Danainae)." *Alexanor* 18 (1993): 189–192.

Tilden, J. W. "Attempted mating between male Monarchs." *Journal of Research On the Lepidoptera* 18 (1981): 2.

Troyer, H. L., Burks, C. S. and Lee, R. E. "Phenology of cold-hardiness in reproductive and migrant Monarch butterflies (*Danaus plexippus*) in southwest Ohio." *Journal of Insect Physiology* 42 (1996): 633–642.

Tuskes, P. M. and Brower, L. P. "Overwintering ecology of the Monarch butterfly, *Danaus plexippus* L., in California." *Ecological Entomology* 3 (1978): 141–153.

Urquhart, F. A. "Fluctuation in the numbers of the Monarch butterfly (*Danaus plexippus*) in North America." *Atalanta* 3 (1970): 104–114.

—. "Fluctuations in Monarch butterfly populations." *News of the Lepidopterists' Society* 1974: 1–2.

—. "Found at last: the Monarch's winter home." *National Geographic Magazine* 150 (1976): 160–173.

—. "Monarch migration studies." *News of the Lepidopterists' Society* 1978: 3–4.

—. "Conservation areas for the eastern population of the Monarch butterfly, *Danaus plexippus plexippus* (Lepidoptera: Danaidae)." *Proceedings of the Entomological Society of Ontario* 110 (1980): 109.

—.; Urquhart, N. R. and Munger, F. "A study of a continuously breeding population of *Danaus plexippus* in southern California compared to a migratory population and its significance in the study of insect movement." *Journal of Research On the Lepidoptera* 7 (1970): 169–181.

Walton, R. K. and Brower, L. P. "Monitoring the Fall Migration of the Monarch Butterfly *Danaus plexippus* L. (Nymphalidae: Dananinae) in Eastern North America: 1991–1994. *Lepidopterists' Society Journal* 50 (1976): 1–20.

Vasconcellos-Neto, J. and Lewinsohn, T. M. "Discrimination and release of unpalatable butterflies by *Nephila clavipes*, a neotropical orb-weaving spider." *Ecological Entomology* 9 (1984): 337–344.

Weiss, S. B. "Forest canopy structure at overwintering Monarch butterfly sites: measurements with hemispherical photography." *Conservation Biology* 5 (1991): 165–175.

Wells, H., Wells, P. H. and Cook, P. "The importance of overwinter aggregations for reproductive success of Monarch butterflies (*Danaus plexippus*)." *Journal of Theoretical Biology* 147 (1990): 115–132.

Wells, H., Strauss, E. G., Rutter, M. A. and Wells, P. H. "Mate location, population growth and species extinction." *Biological Conservation* 86 (1998): 317–324.

Wilson, M. F., Bertin, R. I. and Price, P. W. "Nectar production and flower visitors of *Asclepias verticillata*." *American Midland Naturalist* 192 (1979): 23–35.

Winter, D. "Misdirected Monarch mating behavior (Danaidae: *Danaus plexippus*) or noblesse oblige?" *Journal of the Lepidopterists' Society* 39 (1985): 334.

Yeager, D. "Monarch behaviors in south Texas." *News of the Lepidopterists' Society* 1974: 3.

Young, A. M. "On the evolutionary distance between asclepiadaceous-feeding danaids and apocynaceous-feeding ithomiids." *Journal of Research On the Lepidoptera* 18 (1981): 251–254.

—. "Some differences between temperate and tropical populations of Monarch (*Danaus plexippus*) and queen (*D. gilippus*) butterflies (Lepidoptera: Danaidae)." *Entomol. News* 85 (1974): 116–126.

Zalucki, M. P. and Kitching, R. L. "The dynamics of adult *Danaus plexippus* L. (Danaidae) within patches of its food plant, *Asclepias* spp." *Journal of the Lepidopterists' Society* 38 (1984): 209–219.

Zalucki, M. P. and Suzuki, Y. "Milkweed patch quality, adult population structure, and egg laying in the Monarch butterfly." *Journal of the Lepidopterists' Society* 41 (1987): 13–22.

Zalucki, M. P., Brower, L. P. and Alonso, A. M. "Detrimental effects of latex and cardiac glycosides on survival and growth of first-instar Monarch butterfly larvae, *Danaus plexippus*, feeding on the sandhill milkweed, *Asclepias humistrata*." *Ecological Entomology* 26 (2001): 212–224.

Zangerl, A. R., McKenna, D., Wraight, C.L., Carroll, M., Ficarellow, P., Warner, R. and Berenbaum, M.R. "Effects of exposure to event 176 *Bacillus thuringiensis* corn pollen on Monarch and black swallowtail caterpillars under field conditions." Proceedings of the National Academy of Sciences (Washington) 98 (21) (2001): 11908–11912.

Index

Photo Credits